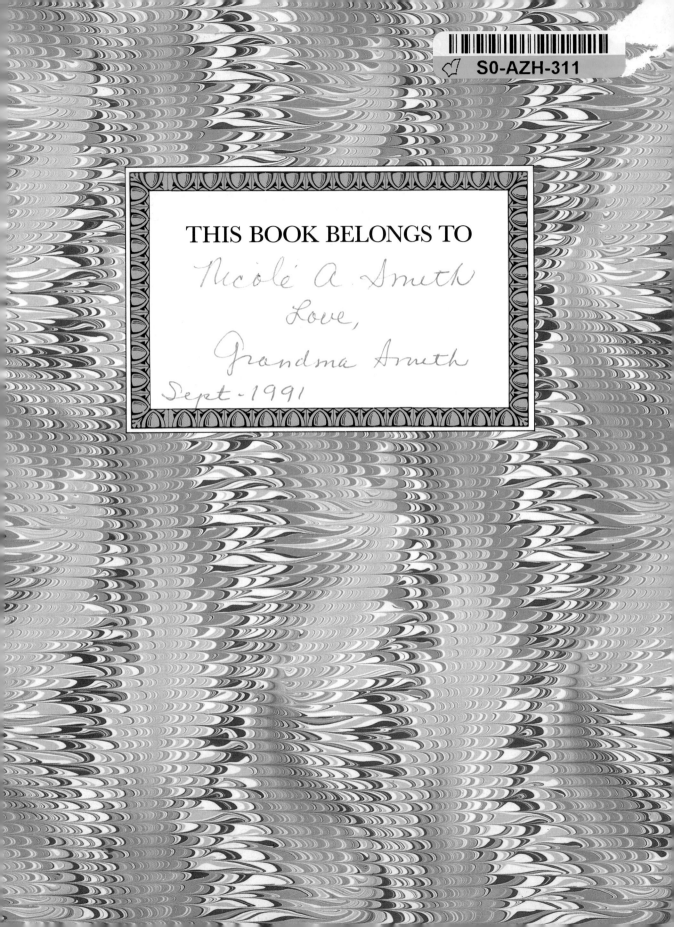

THIS BOOK BELONGS TO

Nicole A. Smith

Love,

Grandma Smith

Sept. 1991

Jesus blesses the children (page 208)

The angel with the flaming sword stood guarding the gates
(page 12)

STORIES FROM
THE
BIBLE

STORIES FROM
THE
BIBLE

Illustrated by Harry G. Theaker

GALLERY BOOKS
An Imprint of W. H. Smith Publishers Inc.
112 Madison Avenue
New York, NY 10016

Gallery Books are available for bulk purchase
for sales promotions and premium use.
For details write or telephone the Manager of
Special Sales, W.H. Smith Publishers, Inc.,
112 Madison Avenue, New York, New York 10016
(212) 532-6600

Typeset by Litho Link Ltd, Welshpool Wales
Printed and bound in Norway

LIST OF ILLUSTRATIONS

THE OLD TESTAMENT

THE NEW TESTAMENT

CONTENTS

PREFACE

This book of special stories has been written for children as an introduction to the greatest and most wonderful story book in the world. The stories chosen are mainly those in which children are themselves the central figures. The tales are hardly more than outlines, for the old tellers of the Bible stories wrote pithily and wasted no words.

However, an effort has been made to picture the setting, to show the children of long ago among the birds and flowers of Canaan, or going on camel-back down the desert road to Shur. For these children were *real* children; little Isaac must have eaten honey made by the wild bees of Judea; Ishmael, who grew up to be an archer in the wilderness, watched the kestrels overhead; and Samuel almost certainly measured his growth by the fit of the little coats his mother made him each year.

Last and best of all, the stories of the Christ child, and of the children whom He loved and blessed, are retold in a way that will stir children and help them understand a way of life far removed from our own.

THE
OLD
TESTAMENT

IN THE
BEGINNING

At the beginning of this book, there is a picture of an angel holding a sword that looks as if it is on fire. Well, this angel was once set to guard the gates of a garden – a garden of wonderful trees. This garden was in a strange, hot country, where you sometimes find miles and miles of wind-tossed sand, and sometimes high, rocky mountains, and sometimes wide rivers that flow between banks of tall reeds. Part of this land was called "The Land of Wandering." In this country there were big cities, once fine and strong, but long since fallen into ruins, with kings' palaces built inside their towered walls.

People who could make beautiful things in silver and gold and brass, who could carve in ivory and shape delicate vases upon potters' wheels lived there. They hunted lions and other wild beasts in the desert, and then came back to banquets where music was played to them as they ate and drank. And at the kings' courts were men who called themselves magicians, and thought that they could read the future in the water, or the sand, or sometimes in the stars.

Away from the great cities, where the kings and princes were often very wicked, lived the people of the Tents. They had sheep and cattle for property, and they moved through the Land of Wandering from place to place. Some of them were very rich and owned beautiful things made of silver and gold, though they did not build temples and houses. The greatest treasure they had, greater than any jewel that ever shone, was their belief in God.

They told of God in all their stories and sang His praise in all their songs. The little dark-haired, dark-eyed boys and girls who played about the tent doors or sat near their mothers at sunset, never tired of hearing the beautiful tales. Some of their grown-up brothers had harps and cymbals, and were taught to make music and to dance, not merely for pleasure, but for worship of the great God to whose people they belonged. Other nations around them prayed to the sun, or the moon, or even to big stone pillars set up in the temples of the hills. But the children of the Tent-people prayed to God alone.

Among other tales, the mothers tried to tell the children the story of how God made the world. They said it was made in Six Wonderful Days – what we call the Creation. Every day, they explained, for six days running, God made something beautiful and new. First of all was Light. And then He made the blue skies and seas, the mountains and the meadows, the waving trees, the sun, moon and stars, the fishes, the singing birds and all the animals, great and small. And on the seventh day He rested, and saw that all the things which He had made were good.

The mothers could not explain these Six Wonderful Days of God, nor say how long or how short they had been. But they told how, on the sixth day, God made man in His own image, and afterwards gave him a beautiful garden to live in, and a fair sweet woman to be his wife.

A river flowed through this blossoming garden, and long afterwards it became four rivers, which watered the sandy country in which the big cities were built much later. But the first crystal springs of the river were in Eden, where God had planted the Garden of Wonderful Trees. How wistfully the Tent-people must have talked of it! Trees of every kind grew there. At noon, the sunshine filtered through boughs laden, they liked to think, with apricots and oranges, figs and mulberries, red-gold pomegranates and purple grapes. The loving kindness of God breathed through the blossoms, and His mercy dropped in the gentle silver dew. And the man and the woman, who were called Adam and Eve, could eat all the fruit in the garden except the fruit of a tree which grew in the midst of the others and was called the Tree of Knowledge of Good and Evil. In the midst of the Garden there was also another wonderful tree, the Tree of Life.

Nobody knows what these two trees were like; but they must have been very beautiful, with cool and tempting fruit. We know that the Tree of Knowledge was pleasant to look at; while the Tree of Life seems to have been in a quiet holy place all alone, as if in its boughs lingered the secrets of God. It has never been described to us, and we can only picture it as a Tree of fragrance and mystery; with songs in it that were not sung by birds, and gentle rustlings that were not made by breezes.

I do not think that Adam and Eve wandered near to the sacred Tree of Life often. But the Tree of Knowledge was in a more open place. One day, Eve was in the garden when she heard a rustle near the tree, and presently, among the waving bushes, she saw the head of a big serpent. It spoke to her, and asked why she was not gathering the fine fruit from the Tree of Knowledge, which was the best fruit of all to eat in the garden, and certainly most tempting.

"God told us not to," answered Eve simply. She was not afraid of the Serpent, but stood looking at it in wonder.

"What would happen to you if you disobeyed Him, do you think?" asked the Serpent.

"We should surely die," said Eve.

"Surely not," the Serpent told her, with a wicked, cunning look in its eyes. "God knows that if you eat that fruit, you will be great and powerful, as He is. That is the reason He has told you not to!"

Eve looked at the Serpent again, and then she looked at the fruit on the Tree. It hung, tempting and fragrant and cool among its pretty leaves. There was such a lot of it too; the Tree almost seemed to bend with its weight. The Serpent went nearer the Tree and drew the branches towards her, rustling and twisting its long shining body among them.

"You would be as powerful and know as much as God Himself," it repeated. "Why don't you pick the fruit and eat it?"

Eve wanted to obey God, but somehow the temptation was too strong. She plucked some of the fruit and ate it guiltily. Then Adam came down the path to see what she was doing, and she gave him some to eat, too. When they had finished eating, they looked at each other. And, all at once, they were miserable and sorry and ashamed, and they hurried away from the Tree and the Serpent, and went to the other end of the garden, wondering why they should be unhappy, instead of becoming clever and powerful, as the Serpent had said they would.

The day wore on, the sun sank, and the garden grew sweet and holy and cool. Then a deeper hush came over it, and a little wind thrilled through the hush, and a Voice spoke, gravely and tenderly, through the soft breeze. Adam and Eve knew that God was in the garden, and they hid themselves more deeply and trembled among the trees. But God called to them and asked why they had hidden themselves, and Adam answered that it was because they were so unhappy and ashamed.

God knew before Adam spoke that they had eaten the fruit from the Tree of Knowledge; nothing else could have taken from them the joy and happiness that would always have been theirs if they had not disobeyed Him. He was very grieved and displeased, and told them they could not live in the garden any longer, for He could not trust them. And He told the Serpent that it, too, must be punished. From that moment on, it would always have to crawl on the ground, instead of being able to lift itself up, as other creatures could. When God had said this, the Serpent crept away, and Adam and Eve went sorrowfully out into the desert. And God put His winged angels at the gate to guard the Tree of Life, so that the man and woman were never able to go back into the garden any more.

This was the story told to the little children of the Tent-people in the Land of Wandering. Many hundreds of years later, a man named Moses, of whom we shall read presently, wrote the story down, and it was put, with many other beautiful tales, in a great book.

This book, called the Book of Genesis, is now a part of the Bible, where, any day, you can read the story for yourselves. For, you see, Moses was inspired by God to tell His people all about the Creation, and to show how light could never have come out of darkness, nor land have been separated from water, nor birds and fishes have lived in air and sea, without the Power of God. And, although it had happened long, long, before his day, Moses was led by God to tell, also, how sorrow and pain came to the man and the woman because they disobeyed God's command. In consequence, they were sent out into the Land of Wandering, far away from the beautiful, cool Garden of Wonderful Trees.

Eve was not afraid of the Serpent (page 16)

The dove came back with an olive branch in her beak
(page 25)

NOAH AND
THE FLOOD

his is another story that the Tent-people told their children long, long ago. Once upon a time, there lived a man called Noah, a name that means "comfort".

He was named Noah when he was a tiny baby because his father believed that, through this little child, his other children would be blessed and helped to make better homes for themselves in the parched and dusty Country of Wandering, where the sun was so hot, and the ground so scorched and dry.

Noah lived a long way from the lost Garden, among the cities of some very greedy and wicked people. As he kept watch from his tents, he must have seen the wicked kings and their nobles hunting wild animals in the desert. When he passed near their palaces, he heard them making feasts to glorify their idols of wood and stone. But Noah clung fast to the true faith – the belief in one great God who had made the heavens and the earth.

One day, when this good and just man was

growing old, God's voice came to him, and Noah listened. The Voice told him that, because of the wickedness of the people, a great flood was to cover the earth, but that God meant to save Noah, and his wife, and his sons and their wives from the great waters. For Noah and his family loved God, and He knew that they would teach His word to their children and grandchildren and even their grandchildren after them.

Noah was told to build a great boat, called an Ark, and to take shelter in it, with his sons, Shem, Ham, and Japheth, and their wives, his daughters-in-law. And into the Ark, he was to take two of every kind of living creature – birds, animals, and insects. He was also to take food for himself, his family, and all the animals, enough to last for many weeks.

If you were to travel now to that faraway country where the rivers Tigris and Euphrates flow, you would see, passing up and down the streams, big barges shaped almost like the arks we have all seen in pictures. In these big barges, animals and people are carried to and fro upon the water. It was a boat such as this that Noah was told to build, only very, very much larger.

This boat was to be made of strong, hard wood and covered with pitch inside and out, so that it would be waterproof. It was to have three levels like a house with an attic – a door in the side, and a window near the top. In addition to the people and the animals, a lot of food had to be stored, so that they would not starve.

So Noah and his sons built this wonderful boat, bigger and more wonderful than any ship that had ever been built before.

Then Noah and his family went inside and waited, with the door open, for the animals to follow. What a wonderful waiting time it must have been! Who can tell in what way news of the coming flood whispered its way across the valleys, and above the mountain tops, through the deep forests and over the foaming rivers, to draw the animals to the Ark that was prepared for them.

But they came, slowly or quickly as the case might be, through the drifting mists, leaving their homes and their companions behind. Can you imagine it all? How a great lion and lioness trod, with soft feet and tawny limbs, over the desert sand to the wondrous boat? How a pair of humming birds, as bright as jewels, flew in through the open door? How, presently, a soft-eyed fawn persuaded his still softer-eyed little doe wife to patter timidly up the plank that led to the entrance; and then how two blue butterflies, with wings like silk, fluttered silently to shelter! And, as night fell, the owls must have flown in with strange cries, and the bats also came, quite noiselessly; while morning would bring the wild ducks, and the rabbits, and the larks. Two by two they came.

And when they were all there, God shut them into the Ark where they would be safe. Then, after seven days, the great rivers rose, the little brooks became torrents, and the marshes turned into lakes. From the clouds the rain fell without stopping. To and fro, to and fro, the Ark floated on the face of the waters, until, at last, after many days, God caused the rain to cease.

So, one morning, in the seventh month, on the seventeenth day of the month, the Ark rested on the top of a high mountain called Ararat, the waters began to go down, and those who were inside the Ark saw the peaks of other mountains above the flood. After forty days, Noah opened the little window and let a raven fly out. Also he sent forth a small, soft dove. The raven, a big, strong bird, went forth to and fro and found it could take care of itself. But the little dove came back and fluttered against the window, and Noah put out his hand and drew her back inside where it was safe.

Then, after a week, he sent the dove out again. Again she came back. But this time she had in her beak an olive leaf that she had plucked from a bough. Noah knew then that the green trees were above water. So, after seven days more, he let the dove fly again. This time, the bird did not come back to the Ark at all.

Then, having waited for the waters to dry, Noah opened the door of the Ark, and he and his wife, and his sons and their wives, went out onto the top of the high mountain in the morning light; and the animals followed them. And there, instead of wide rivers with hot deserts spreading out on every side, were green valleys and waving forests, and hill paths bright with flowers. So Noah built an altar on the mountain top and gave thanks to God for bringing them to this beautiful land.

While Noah was offering thanks, God's voice came to him through the mists, promising that He would never destroy the entire world by flood again, but that, while the earth remained, planting time and harvest, cold and heat, summer and winter, day and night, should not cease. And God told Noah to cultivate the earth, and bade him look for the token of the promise in the clouds.

As Noah looked, he saw beautiful gleaming hues

group and gather in the mists of the dawn. They rose high in a shining semi-circle over the mountain. And Noah, looking at the rainbow, and remembering his deliverance, knelt again in adoration and thankfulness.

THE LITTLE PRINCE OF THE WILDERNESS

he years passed, and after a time, a great man grew up in the country that had once been covered with the waters of the Flood. He was at first called Abram; in later years God told him he must change his name to Abraham, because that meant a father of many nations. Abraham left the land where he was born and went to live in Canaan, which we call the Holy Land today. After many wanderings, he set up his tents in the plain of Mamre, near Hebron, and lived there with his wife, Sarah, his little son, Ishmael, and Ishmael's mother, who was called Hagar, a brown-eyed, dark-haired Egyptian.

Abraham and Sarah had brought Hagar back from Egypt after a long trip they had once made there; and Sarah, who had no children of her own, was very glad, at first, that Abraham and Hagar had a little son. Abraham was a sort of Shepherd-King, who had much gold and silver, and many flocks of cattle and sheep. Unless he had a son of his own, all these things would pass away from his family at his death. Then, too, Sarah knew that God had promised her husband that he should be the father of a great nation. So she thought that, through Ishmael, Abraham's name would be carried on.

They all lived contentedly together until, at last, Sarah had a baby of her own who was named Isaac. She knew, by this, that God had blessed her and Abraham very greatly. Abraham loved Sarah's tiny son very, very dearly, but he still loved the lad Ishmael as well. It seemed that they might have gone on in happiness if only Ishmael had been kind to the baby and loved this soft, helpless little brother.

But Ishmael was a wild, thoughtless boy, probably always wanting to shoot arrows among the rocks, and at the hawks overhead. He was rather jealous to tell the truth, about the fuss that everybody made over the new baby. When Abraham and Sarah had a big splendid feast to celebrate tiny Isaac's birth, Ishmael laughed out loud at the whole thing – and laughed at the new baby most of all.

Sarah saw him laughing and was very angry – so angry that she forgot the time when she had been glad that Abraham and Hagar had a little son. She went and told Abraham, and asked him to send both Ishmael and his mother away. For she said, "Hagar is only an Egyptian slave, after all, and I am a princess of the shepherd-kings and have given you a son of your own family and tribe."

Abraham listened with a sad heart. He did not know what to do. He loved Ishmael; but he saw that the boy would never be kind to Isaac, and that Sarah would always be unhappy and vexed. And he worried very much about it, until God's voice came to him in the night and comforted him:

The voice told him to do as Sarah had said, but it gave a promise that, although it must be Isaac who would carry on Abraham's name and inherit his shepherd-kingdom, yet Ishmael also would be greatly blessed and have twelve princes for his sons. So Abraham was comforted, for he knew that he could safely send Hagar away. She would have God as her Protector, to look after her and her young son.

So, while Sarah and Isaac were still asleep in the tent, and only the early cries of the goatherds and the soft bleating of sheep and lowing of cattle could be heard on the plain outside, Abraham rose and went out in search of Hagar. He found her in her own tent with Ishmael, not knowing what was going to happen. Very sorrowfully, yet knowing that harm could not come to them, he bade the Egyptian woman and her son goodbye. Giving Hagar as much bread as she could carry and setting a big bottle of water on her shoulder, he sent her into the wilderness, with Ishmael, laughing and lighthearted as ever, running before her.

Abraham watched, in grief and yet in hope, until they were out of sight. Then he turned back to his own tent. He prayed to God for them while the mother and son went on in the beautiful clear air of the morning, which made the sands of the desert glisten like diamonds, and showed up the high brown rocks, all sharp and dark against the blue sky.

Hagar, perhaps hardly thinking what she did, turned her steps towards the great sandy track that led from Canaan, through the desert of Beersheba, into Egypt, the land of her birth. Down this track, large groups of people, called "caravans", often came and went, with camels, and covered wagons, and teams of mules shaking their sweet-toned bridle bells. Perhaps Hagar thought that she might meet such a caravan going down to Egypt with timber, or sheep skins, or even rare woven carpets for sale. If she met one, they would most likely be kind to her, and give her and Ishmael help upon their hard and lonely way.

Once before, she had been down the same desert road. Long, long ago, before Ishmael was born,

Sarah had one day been angry with the Egyptian girl-slave. Hagar had been ungrateful, even though Sarah had been kind. So Hagar had run away from Abraham and his wife, and had been found by an angel near a well on her way back to Egypt. The angel had told her to return to her kind master and mistress and to obey Sarah. At the same time, this messenger from God had promised that Ishmael would soon be born.

Very likely, Hagar was thinking of this, and trying to find her way along the caravan trail to the same well. But somehow she wandered in the wrong direction and got lost in the great, hot, lonely desert. Ishmael, after being so cheerful and brave, grew faint and weary. All the water in the bottle had been drunk, so that Hagar could not give him anything to quench his thirst or cool his parched throat and tongue.

On and on they wandered, over the scorching sand, until at last, poor, weary, stricken Hagar broke down. She laid Ishmael in the slight shade of a little bush and went a good way off. "For," she said to herself brokenly, "I cannot bear to watch the death of my child."

Then kneeling down in the weary desert, with the wild animals not far away among the rocks, and the cruel vultures hanging overhead, she broke into deep and bitter sobbing. But suddenly, as she sobbed, an angel's voice called to her, softly and clearly, from the sky.

"Hagar, what aileth thee? Fear not! For God hath heard the voice of the lad where he is!"

"Arise! Lift up the lad and hold him in thine arms! For I will make him a great nation!"

Hagar hushed her weeping and listened. The angel's voice died away; but, in the silence, she heard a wonderful sound instead – the soft ripple of cool water, bubbling up through the hot sand. Then God opened her eyes, and she saw that she was kneeling quite close to a sparkling well. She filled the empty bottle with water again, and went joyfully across to Ishmael, and have him a long, cool drink.

God kept the promise that He had given both to Abraham, far away in his tent in Mamre, and to Hagar, sitting in the desert by the well. Ishmael grew up brave and strong, and became a great archer in the wilderness.

When he was grown Hagar chose for him a wife from Egypt – a brown-eyed, dark-haired maiden, just as Hagar herself had been when she was young. And they had many sons and daughters, princes and princesses of the wilderness, like Ishmael and his wife.

themselves. And they lived in harmony as a family.

Isaac and Ishmael met again one day, and remembered that they were brothers. That was on the day when they buried their good and faithful old father Abraham, laying him to rest in the quiet shadows of a great cave near the plain of Mamre, where already Sarah, his wife, had rested for many years. Isaac, too, was married by that time to a kind and beautiful woman called Rebekah, who had comforted him after his mother's death. Ishmael lived, wild and free, in the desert, but Isaac grew up from babyhood among the tents of his father, the shepherd-king. Our next story is about something that happened to Isaac when he was a little boy.

ISAAC AND THE
BEAUTIFUL ANGEL

One warm night in the plain of Mamre, when the stars were shining like great lamps in the deep blue-black heavens, and the wind, sweet and silky-dry, was blowing over the closed flowers, Abraham lay asleep in the cool, dark shelter of his tent. It must have been a nice tent, as suited the greatness of a shepherd-king; the carpets would have been soft and the hangings warm and fine. All was peaceful, when suddenly, through the stillness of the tent, a voice sounded. And the voice was that of God.

"Abraham," said the voice. "Abraham!"

Abraham woke instantly. "Behold!" he answered. "Here I am!"

Then the voice told him to do what seemed a very strange and terrible thing.

"Take now thy son, thine only son Isaac, whom thou lovest," came the sad words through the darkness, "and get thee unto the land of Moriah. And offer him there as a burnt offering upon one of the mountains which I will tell thee of."

The voice ceased, but Abraham, startled and bewildered, made no reply. Sacrifice his little son Isaac! The child for whose sake he had parted with Ishmael, and whom he loved better than all the world! How was he to do this thing? Yet God had spoken. And Abraham had never failed to obey.

So, when morning broke, all brilliant in soft rose lights over the eastern hills, he rose from his bed and went out into the beautiful dawn – just as he had gone out to waken Hagar and Ishmael a few years before. He saddled one of his donkeys and called two of the young shepherds who were his servants. Then he went to rouse his little son, Isaac, from sleep.

Isaac slept near his mother Sarah, and there is no doubt that her tent would have been very beautiful for she was a great princess among the shepherd-kings. She would have had purple curtains, and a silver hanging lamp burning fragrant oil, and Isaac would most likely have slept on a soft mattress that, in those days, was used as a bed.

The little boy woke quickly and was pleased to follow his father into the clear light of the dewy morning. They went down with the young shepherds to cut some wood – perhaps from almond or fir-trees. Abraham and his servants chopped the boughs, while Isaac looked on eagerly. He knew that his father was going to offer a sacrifice to God, and I dare say he was very pleased and proud because he was allowed to help.

You know, in those days so long ago, the people in the land where Abraham lived would sometimes give what they called a burnt-offering to God. They would kill a goat or a lamb – quite quickly, so that it felt no pain – and then lay it on an altar built of stones, and put branches of wood all around it, and set the wood on fire. This was known as a "sacrifice."

So the sad shepherd-king seated his little son in front of him on the donkey and the two servants took the wood, and they set off, in sorrowful procession, towards the distant hill of Moriah. It was a three-day journey, and oh! so different from the usual way in which Isaac journeyed with his father. Usually, they sat on stately camels, with fine tents in wagons drawn by oxen, and with servants to wait on them and to prepare food and shelter at night. But Isaac understood that this was a sort of holy journey, to be made in humble obedience and devotion to God.

The road they took was in exactly the opposite direction from that which Hagar had taken with little Ishmael. So, instead of going along the hot desert road towards Egypt, they journeyed among craggy rocks and through stony valleys with wild shrubs

Hagar and her son Ishmael went forth into the wilderness
(page 30)

Abraham and his son Isaac climbed the path together
(page 41)

growing here and there. They saw young deer feeding among the scattered patches of grass and heard the loud humming of the bees. There would have been wild hill goats, too, leaping up the mountain sides, and little foxes and jackals that lived in rocky holes. Always they went uphill, towards the high mountain in the distance, with its dark heights and silvery olive groves.

You may be quite sure that little Isaac enjoyed this new and wonderful journey, but Abraham must have been very downcast and sad. He went on steadily, however, and then, on the third day, he lifted up his eyes and saw the place for the sacrifice afar off.

The little procession had just reached the top of a barren hill, where the wind blew strong and free. In front of them was a long plain, with a range of hills to the east. And at the end of the plain rose the steep slopes of Mount Moriah.

Long, long afterwards, a beautiful Temple, about which you will read later, was built on Mount Moriah. But, when Abraham saw it afar off, it was just a great, lonely hill covered with olive groves. Not very far away was a half-hidden, mysterious city called Salem, which Abraham had visited some years before. In this mysterious city there lived a priest-king who had a strange long name – Melchizedek –

and who prayed to God. He had blessed Abraham at Salem and had brought bread and wine to give him; it was at a time when Abraham had helped to drive away the enemies of the priest-king.

But now Abraham, chief of the shepherds, was just a lonely, weary, sorrowful pilgrim, instead of a conquering prince of God, as the priest-king had called him. And no mighty priest came forth from Salem, with bread and wine, to meet him. All alone, without help or comfort, he must go forward to Moriah, to do as God had told him.

So he said to the young servants, "Abide ye here with the donkey, and the boy and I will go yonder and worship, and come again to you." Then he took the wood of the burnt-offering and gave it to Isaac, his son. In his hand he took the little vessel that held the charcoal-fire and a knife, and he and Isaac went away, both together, down into the stony plain towards the mountain at the end.

For a little while, they walked along the rocky path in silence, with the sound of the wind around them. High above the sides of the eastern hills, the sun had risen and was now shining, bright and beautiful, upon the sad father and his wondering son. Little Isaac felt awed. He seemed to know that something sad and dreadful was going to happen.

At last he looked up, and said, in a troubled voice, "My father?" And Abraham answered gravely, "Here am I, my son." Then Isaac, still more troubled, said, "Behold the fire and the wood! But where is the lamb for the burnt-offering?"

Then Abraham's face grew set and almost stern in its anguish. But all he answered was: "My son, God Himself will provide a lamb for the burnt-offering!"

And then they went on in silence again.

At last they came to the foot of Mount Moriah and, side by side, climbed the steep path that led to the top. Little Isaac was silent and wistful now, and Abraham spoke not a word. When they reached the summit of the hill, still in silence, Abraham built an altar, small and square, of the stones that lay scattered around. Everything on the mountain was still, and the wild red deer and the upland goats stood watchful and silent upon the high rocks, while the pretty deer drew back with their fawns into the dark olive groves. From Salem, perhaps, came strange, faint music – the songs and cymbals of the morning sacrifice offered by the priestly king. But Isaac and his father were quite alone.

Then, when Abraham had built the altar, he laid the wood in order, and he took his little son Isaac, bound him, and laid him on the altar and upon the wood. Then he stretched out his hand and took the knife to slay his son.

Isaac had not spoken or moved. He had just looked into his father's face and wondered, pitifully, what it all meant. Then, just as Abraham took the knife in his hand, a high, clear call came ringing over the mountain, a call that seemed to drop straight from the sky.

"Abraham! Abraham!" came the call.

The shepherd-king, still with the knife in his hand, began to tremble. Yet he answered bravely, "Here am I!"

Then the angel of the Lord said, "Lay not thine hand upon the child, neither do thou anything unto him! For now I know that thou fearest God, seeing that thou hast not withheld thy son, thine only son."

Abraham was oh! so glad and happy that little Isaac was saved. So now he unbound the child and lifted him to the ground, and they gave thanks together. And then Abraham lifted up his eyes, and looked, and lo! behind him was a ram – one of the wild mountain sheep – caught in a thicket by his horns. So Abraham went and took the ram, and offered it as a burnt offering in place of his son.

Abraham gave that place the name "Jehovah-jireh," which means "God will see, or provide."

Long afterwards, on the two hills of Zion and Moriah, was built the city of Jeru-salem, where the Lord Jesus Christ taught in the Temple and showed the glory of God. But, once upon a time, Moriah had been just the great wooded hill where the angel saved little Isaac, and told his earthly father of the watchful love of the Father of Heaven.

The angel called to Abraham from heaven a second time, after the ram had been offered, and told him, how pleased God was with him for his faithful obedience, and because he had not held back his previous little son, Isaac. And the angel repeated the promise God had made to Abraham before Isaac was born, that his children and grandchildren and great-grandchildren should be as many as the stars of the heaven or as the sand upon the seashore.

JOSEPH AND HIS BROTHERS

You remember that Isaac had married a beautiful woman named Rebekah, who made him very happy. You can read all about her and her marriage in the Bible; and also about her son Jacob, and *his* wife Rachel, with whom he fell deeply in love when he met her bringing her father's sheep to drink at a big well. Now I am going to tell you the story of the two sons of Jacob and Rachel, who were named Joseph and Benjamin, and who were born when Jacob was growing old.

Jacob had another name, Israel, which means "a prince of God." Abraham, too, had been called God's prince once, by some people known as the children of Heth, who had sold him a field for a burying-place. People from many nations owned land in Canaan. They built cities there, long ago destroyed and forgotten, like the mysterious city of Salem on the hill opposite Mount Moriah. But the shepherd-princes – Abraham, Isaac, and Jacob – built no cities. They moved from place to place with their servants and their great flocks of sheep and cattle. Sometimes, where they set up their tents, they bought the land from the kings. These kings did not worship God in the same way that the shepherds did, but they respected the shepherds and would always sell a piece of land to those of them with whom they were friendly.

Well, Jacob, whose other name was Israel, wandered from place to place with his flocks and his servants, until at last, when Joseph was a boy and Benjamin a tiny baby, he settled down in the very spot where his grandfather Abraham had set up his tents long, long ago. This was, you remember, among the green fields of Mamre, in Hebron, and Abraham and Isaac were both buried there. Rachel was dead, too. But, for her sweet sake, Jacob loved Joseph and Benjamin far better than the sons of Leah, who had been his first wife.

He could not help loving Joseph, the son of his old age, for Joseph was a bright, clever boy, who had a warm, kind heart for tiny Benjamin. One day, to show how much he thought of Joseph, and that he meant this younger son to be a mighty chief, Jacob gave the boy a beautiful new coat. It was woven in all the shades of the rainbow, and it floated about him like the cloak of a great prince as he walked on the hills with his long shepherd's staff in his hand. When his brothers saw Joseph in this gleaming coat, they were angry and jealous, and could not speak peaceably to him at all.

One night, Joseph had a strange dream. Excited and wondering, he ran to his brothers to tell them about it.

"Hear!" he said. "Hear, I pray you, this dream that I have dreamed.

"Behold, we were binding sheaves of grain in a field, and lo! my sheaf arose and stood upright! And, behold, your sheaves stood up, too, all around, and bent down before my sheaf!"

He could not help thinking that it was a very wonderful dream. Picture it yourselves: the sunlit field of corn; the big sheaves lying on the ground, with all the brothers tying them ready to be put into the stack. And then imagine Joseph's sheaf rising up, and the brothers' sheaves doing the same, gathering around in a ring and bending in homage to Joseph's sheaf, while everybody in the cornfield stood silent and amazed!

But his brothers were angry. "Shalt thou indeed reign over us?" they said. And they hated him even more.

Then Joseph had a second dream. He dreamed he

was alone in the deep sky, and behold! The sun and the moon and eleven stars paid reverence to him. This time, he told the dream to his father, as well as to his brothers, but his father rebuked him, and said:

"What is this dream that thou hast dreamed? Shall I and thy mother and thy brethren indeed come to bow down ourselves to thee to the earth?"

But, although Jacob rebuked Joseph, he thought about the dream. The eleven brothers, however, envied and disliked Joseph more than ever.

Some time before this, Jacob had bought a large piece of land on the other side of Mount Moriah. The place was called Shechem, and there he had sunk a deep well. Soon after the nights when Joseph had dreamed his strange dreams, the eleven brothers went on a journey to Shechem, where their father had many sheep and cattle out at pasture. Jacob, who, as you know, was now an old man, stayed behind in Hebron. One day, he called Joseph and told him to go to Shechem and see how his brothers and the flocks were faring.

So Joseph set off on his travels, which would take him past that very mountain where Abraham and Isaac had heard the voice of the angel many years before. But after four or five days, when he got to Shechem, he saw only the wide rolling pastures looking lonely and empty in the sunshine. The big stone covered the mouth of the well, and no flocks lay around it, as they usually did in the morning and evening, waiting for the shepherds to roll away the stone and fill the long troughs with water from their goat-skin buckets. There was nobody but one man, a solitary wanderer like Joseph himself. This man was able to tell him that his brothers had taken the flocks to new feeding grounds, a little farther away.

So Joseph went in the direction of the place the man had described. Presently, in the distance, he saw the clustered tents and heard the soft bleating of the sheep and the lowing of the cattle. He hurried forward to greet his brothers. But they had seen him afar off, and they hated him as much as ever.

"Behold this dreamer cometh!" they said mockingly. "Let us kill him and throw him into some pit. We can say that a wild beast has devoured him! And then we shall see what becomes of his dreams!"

But one of the brothers, Reuben, was kinder than the rest. He felt that he must save Joseph's life. So he suggested that they should throw him into a pit, but should not spill his blood. And he thought that, when the others were gone, he would come back and rescue the boy and send him home to their father.

So when Joseph, pleased and proud after his

journey, came eagerly to greet his brothers, they took hold of him roughly, stripped his beautiful coat from his shoulders, and threw him into an empty pit near-by. Then they sat down to eat their supper.

As they were eating, there came, stepping slowly and proudly down the distant road, a long procession of camels, sending out their soft shadows over the ground, and creating a wonderful dark picture against the clear blue sky. On the backs of the camels were big loads of spices and balm and myrrh. The camels were coming from Gilead, which was a grassy country on the other side of the River Jordan, which had many different kinds of plants growing in the rich soil. The men to whom the camels belonged were a company of Ishmaelites — the grandchildren and great-grandchildren of Ishmael and his Egyptian wife, conquerors and princes of the desert, who journeyed up and down its long stretches, carrying spices and gums to sell in Egypt, and bringing back fine cotton cloth in return.

Then Judah, another brother, said, "Let us not slay our brother, but let us sell him to these traders as a slave. Then shall our hand not be upon him. For he is our brothers and our flesh."

The brothers agreed to this, and they pulled Joseph up out of the pit again and sold him to the

Ishmaelites for twenty pieces of silver. So the beloved young son of Israel was taken away by the Ishmaelites, seated on one of the big brown camels. And the procession, with the strange sweet song of the drivers, and the ceaseless tinkling of the bridle bells, passed away from the meadows of Shechem, where the wild flowers blossomed and the sheep and cattle fed, and went swinging away towards the great desert track that led down to Egypt, along the very road where Hagar had wept over Ishmael in the wilderness on the way to Shur.

But when Reuben, who had not been there when Joseph was sold, went to the pit and found that the boy was gone, he ripped his clothes in grief. Then the cruel brothers killed a kid, dipped poor Joseph's fine coat in it, and took the coat, all covered with blood, back to Hebron, and showed it to Jacob, telling him that they had found it. And Jacob, like Reuben, tore his clothes and wept.

"An evil beast has killed my young son Joesph," he said. "I shall go in mourning to my grave."

But, all the time, Joseph was safe with the traders on the big camels, and the Ishmaelites, when they reached Egypt, sold him to a rich man named Potiphar, who was an official in the court of the Pharaoh, a great Egyptian king.

"MY BROTHER
BENJAMIN!"

What a change it must have been for Joseph! Potiphar, his master, soon saw that there was something fine and upright in everything that the young shepherd from Canaan did. He saw, too, that he was clever and clear-headed. As time went on, he gave him a great deal of authority, and let him have almost full charge of all his money and goods. But one day a false and cruel story was told to Potiphar about the youth he trusted. Potiphar believed it, and, in his anger, put Joseph into the King's prison, over which, as Pharaoh's chief officer, he had command.

But, even in prison, Joseph made friends; the very keeper of the prison soon began to trust him, just as Potiphar had done. The lad was so fearless and honest and upright that everybody saw he followed the ways of the true God. The other thing that interested all the Egyptians about him very much was that he could explain the meaning of dreams.

Among his fellow prisoners at one time were

Pharaoh's chief butler and chief baker, who had both been put in prison for wrongdoing. They had strange dreams one night, and Joseph told them what the dreams meant. That of the butler ended happily – Joseph told him it meant that the King would forgive him. And, surely enough, after a few days, Pharaoh sent for his servant, pardoned him, and gave him back his old place in the royal household.

Well, after a little time had passed, Pharaoh himself had a curious dream. He thought he saw seven fine fat cows feeding in a meadow. Then up out of the river came seven thin cows, looking, oh! so strange as they rose from the waters! And they ate all the fat cattle up!

Pharaoh awoke, wondering. By and by he fell asleep again, and again he dreamed. This time, he saw seven ears of corn, yellow and full, upon one stalk. Then another stalk, with seven thin, wind-blasted ears, sprang up alongside. And the thin ears ate the good ears up.

In the morning, the King sent for his magicians and asked the meaning of his dreams, but they could not tell him. Then the chief butler remembered Joseph in the prison and told Pharaoh about the Canaanite shepherd who could explain dreams. So the King sent for Joseph in haste. And Joseph stood before this mighty ruler of Egypt and explained what the dream meant.

"Both dreams are one," he said. "The seven cows and the seven ears of corn each mean seven years. By these dreams God has shown Pharaoh that there shall be, first seven years of plentiful harvests in Egypt, and then seven years of famine. And the grievous famine shall eat up all that was stored in the time of plenty. God has shown Pharaoh the King what He means to do. So let the King look for a discreet and wise man, and give him power to store up the harvests of the good years ready for the days of want."

Then Pharaoh answered Joseph: "Forasmuch as God hath showed thee all this, there is none so discreet and wise as thou art. See! I have set *thee* over all the land of Egypt!"

He placed his own ring on Joseph's hand, put a gold chain around his neck, and gave him clothes to wear that were even more beautiful than the wonderful coat of long ago.

So Joseph was given the power to store the harvests during the seven years of plenty, and, when the days of famine came, to distribute the corn that had been put away. And, in those sad and hungry days, a most strange and wonderful thing happened.

Jacob, his old father, sent the brothers of Joseph down into Egypt to buy corn!

You see, the famine was in the land of Canaan, too, but news came that the Egyptians, under the wise guardianship of a good and discreet man, had stored a great deal of corn and would sell it to other nations. So Jacob sent his ten sons to buy. But Benjamin, his youngest, who had taken the place of Joseph in his love, he would not trust to leave him.

So the ten brothers came to Joseph in his palace and bowed down before him, just as the sheaves of grain had bowed down in the dream, long, long ago. They begged him to sell them food.

When Joseph saw them, the memory of Canaan, and of his shepherd-father, and of his brother Benjamin, rushed over him. And he had to turn away from them to weep. But the brothers had no idea that this rich and splendid man, was the boy they had sold to the Ishmaelites in the days of old.

So Joseph let them have some corn, although he pretended not to trust them. He questioned them roughly and heard that they had a younger brother called Benjamin. He told them that next time they came they must bring Benjamin with them, or he would not sell them anything at all. Yet, when they went away, he had all their money put back into the

His brothers pulled Joseph up out of the pit (page 49)

Judah brought Benjamin and presented him to Joseph
(page 57)

tops of their sacks of grain without telling them.

The famine was very bad in Canaan, and, once again, Jacob told his sons to go and buy food in Egypt. But they said it was of no use to go without Benjamin. At last, after long persuasion, and because Judah, one of the brothers, promised to make sure the boy was safe, Jacob let his beloved son go.

Joseph, when he heard that they were in Egypt again, had them brought to his own house and prepared a banquet for them. Then Judah brought Benjamin and presented him to Joseph. After a minute or two of gazing upon his younger brother's face, Joseph was obliged to go away by himself again and weep for love and joy.

They all sat down at the banquet, but Joseph was at the master's table, by himself. But he kept sending delicious dishes to his brothers, who, to their great surprise, found themselves seated at the table according to their ages. The nicest of all the dishes were sent to Benjamin, and he had five times as much as any of his brothers. When the brothers went away with their corn, Joseph again had their money put into the tops of their sacks. But in Benjamin's sack he put not only money, but his own beautiful silver cup.

Then he sent servants after them, saying that his

silver cup had been stolen, and that, whoever had hidden it in his sack must come back and be his slave. And behold! the cup was found in the sack that belonged to Benjamin!

So they all came back to Joseph's house and fell on their faces before him. Judah begged that Benjamin should be released and offered to become a slave in his stead.

Then Joseph could bear it no longer. He sent all the Egyptians away and told his brothers that he was Joseph, the son of their own father, Jacob also known as Israel. And he bade them to bring their father to Egypt and promised that Pharaoh the King, his master, would be very good to them all.

With great joy, they went back to Canaan and brought Jacob, the old man, to see his son, who was alive and found again.

So, once more, Jacob embraced Joseph, the son of his old age. And he was presented to the mighty Egyptian King, who bent low before the aged shepherd-king to receive his blessing. Pharaoh then gave to the children of Jacob the land of Goshen in which to feed their flocks. And this land, where the grass was sweet and good, with palm trees waving above the grain fields, belonged to the Israelites and their children for many, many years.

THE BABY IN
THE BULRUSHES

ears passed and Pharaoh died. Then Joseph died, and after a long, long time, another Pharaoh came to the throne of Egypt, who knew nothing about Joseph. He became frightened when he saw the great number of Israelites who had grown up in Goshen, and how rich and clever they were, and how they prayed to a wonderful, powerful, unseen God, quite different from the gods of the Egyptians. The new Pharaoh called his ministers to him and told them of his fears.

"Look at all these Hebrew men and women who call themselves the children of Israel," he said. "Who was Israel? I do not know. Do you?"

The ministers looked at each other and shook their heads. They, also, had forgotten or had never heard of Joseph.

"Well, whoever he was, he was not an Egyptian," said the King. "He was a stranger who came and settled here with his relations, and they have grown into large families, and some day, if there is a war, they are likely to join the enemy and become our masters. We must do the only wise thing and make them our servants.

"We must force them to help to build my two beautiful treasure cities – Pithom and Ramses" said the King. "And they must burn clay into bricks that I can use to strengthen my great wall of Shur – the wall that keeps out those desert-princes and their followers to whom the people of Israel probably belong. Go, and arrange that this shall be done!"

So men called "taskmasters" were put over the children of Israel, whose lives were made sadly cruel and hard. Once they had been the owners of everything in Goshen and had lived happily and comfortably in their tents among their own belongings, reaping their field of grain, gathering their crops of dates, and taking care of their flocks of sheep and goats. But now they were no longer their own masters. They had to work very hard for the Egyptians; and, if they worked slowly and unwillingly, they were driven with whips. Very likely some of them had to live, too, in poor little villages built of clay, where they must have been unhappy. Yet, such a number of sturdy boys and girls were born in the poor little homes that Pharaoh said that the Israelites were still a danger so all the little boy babies must be thrown into the River Nile, though the little girl babies, who could never be soldiers when they were grown, could be allowed to live.

This decree was a terrible thing for the Israelites, but they had no power to prevent it. Two kind women – one called Shiphrah, which means beauty, and the other called Puah, which means splendid – tried to save the babies, but all the rest of the Egyptians were eager to please the cruel King. So, whenever they heard of the birth of an Israelite boy, they hurried to the father's home, dragged the poor mite from its mother, and took it away and threw it into the river. Almost every day, the men of the Israelites, as they went to work past the sad women in the early morning, would try to shut their ears to the sobbing of the poor mothers, inside the tents or houses, who had lost their sweet little baby boys.

Then one day an Israelite named Amram, who belonged to the family named Levi, married a woman of the same family or tribe, whose name was Jochebed, which, some people think means "God is glorious." Amram and Jochebed lived among their own people in Goshen, where the palms grew, perhaps in a tent, or perhaps in a little clay house. They could see the towers of the great city called Ramses not very far away and watch the distant sails of the big boats that sailed up and down the River Nile, as they still do today. Such strange sails they were! Sometimes white, and sometimes red, they were always sloping to one side as if they were blown by a high wind. Near the river were the waving fields of barley, and overhead was the hot, wide, blue sky.

As time went on, a little daughter was born to Amram and Jochebed, whom they named Miriam. She grew up to be a very clever and sensible little girl, but she must always have been rather sad, for she would see her father go off every morning to work for the Egyptians, while all around her in the sorrowful homes were the poor mothers whose boy babies had been snatched from them and thrown into the cruel waters of the Nile. Then, at last, one day, Jochebed had a little boy baby herself!

He was such a beautiful baby – soft and round, with satiny skin and little curls on his head, and eyes like diamonds.

How Miriam loved the baby! How terrified she was that he might be taken from them – how thankful and glad when Jochebed said she was going to save the beautiful child if she possibly could. Earnestly, Miriam helped her mother to hide the baby; and, for three months, nobody guessed that he was in the little house. Perhaps the people nearby, who were

Israelites, suspected something, but they never told. He grew big and strong and lovelier than ever. Then one day, Jochebed told Miriam that she was afraid they could not hide him any more, and that they would have to trust him utterly to the care of God.

In Egypt, even today, the peasant women are able to swim across the Nile when they want to get from one side to the other. If a mother has to take her baby with her, she puts the little one into a special basket made of bulrushes and smeared with a gum to keep out the water. Then she shuts the lid carefully, slides the basket into the river, and swims across, pushing the basket in front of her like a safe warm little boat.

So Jochebed took one of these baskets – arks, they are called – and put her baby into it. Then Miriam helped her to carry it down the sandy road and through the cornfields and ricefields, until they came to the river's edge. Graceful reeds and grasses grew there, waving softly in the light of the afternoon sun. The Bible does not describe it, but we know that, just beside the water, was a special pool, with shady trees and floating lilies, in which the Princess, Pharaoh's daughter, came to bathe. It was close to this royal pool that Jochebed planned to leave the baby. Very quietly, she put the basket down on the edge of the water among the waving reeds. Then, with one long last look at the little one, she shut the lid and turned away.

Miriam stayed behind to watch, while Jochebed walked steadily homeward with her eyes fixed on the sky. Somehow she knew that God had shown her what to do with the baby, and He would send somebody to take care of him.

Miriam, meanwhile, hidden among the tall rushes, listened earnestly in case the baby should cry. But the baby was asleep. The sun sank lower and lower, and still the baby slept. Then there came the sound of horses, and wheels, and men calling to the peasants to keep out of the way. Presently, a sort of quietness fell, and women's laughter and voices floated over the water. Miriam, peeping out, saw the Egyptian princess come with her maidens to bathe in the royal pool in the cool of the evening.

As Miriam watched, she saw the princess begin to take off her beautiful robes and hand them to her attendants, some of whom remained near, while others walked along the bank. All at once, the princess caught sight of the basket, and in amazement, stopped undressing. She called to one of her maidens to bring the basket to her.

When the lid was lifted, the baby woke. He saw strange faces around him, instead of those of Miriam and his mother, and he began to cry. The princess looked at him and said:

"This is one of the Hebrew babies – he belongs to the children of Israel."

As she spoke, she noticed that an anxious, eager little girl had crept up and was watching her earnestly. The princess, who was kind and good, smiled at the little girl and then lifted the baby into her own arms.

"I think I shall have to adopt him," she went on. "But who will nurse him for me, if I do? I cannot take him home with me – but somehow I cannot leave him here."

Then Miriam, breathless and bright-eyed, came a little closer.

"Shall I go and find a nurse among the Hebrew women?" she asked very earnestly. "Someone who will nurse the baby for you?"

The princess smiled again, and said, "Go." And she stayed with the baby in her arms until Miriam hurried back, bringing with her Jochebed herself!

Jochebed's face was very happy and very quiet. She said nothing, but looked from the baby to the princess, and back from the princess to the baby. And then Pharaoh's daughter said:

"Take this child away and nurse it for me, and I

will give you your wages."

Jochebed bent very low before the princess and took her own baby back into her arms. Then she and Miriam and the baby went home together.

So now they had no need to hide the little boy, for everybody knew that he was the adopted child of the daughter of the King.

When he grew old enough to do without his mother's daily care, Jochebed took him one day to show the princess what a fine lad he had become. Then Pharaoh's daughter said he must be left with her, to live now at the King's palace, and to be like a son to her. She said: "I will call him Moses, which means 'drawn out,' because I drew him out of the water."

So Moses grew up in the same wonderful King's palace that had sheltered Joseph years ago. When he was a man, he saved the children of Israel from the cruel Egyptian kings.

He who wrote down the stories you have read in this book so far, and many, many more.

MOSES AND THE STAFF OF GOD

Many years later, Moses, now a grown man, stood at the foot of a great mountain that rose out of the golden sands of the desert into the deep blue of the Eastern sky. Stretches of green pasture lay among the bare places. Here and there bushes of wild, white broom could be seen. Little shepherd boys wandered with flocks of sheep and plucked the broom flowers to feed the ewes and lambs. The sheep belonged to Jethro, the Priest of Midian, whose daughter was the wife of Moses. Moses had been obliged to flee from Pharaoh's palace long, long before. He had killed a man who was beating one of the poor, oppressed Israelites, and he had been compelled to leave Egypt forever, as he thought, in fear of his life.

So Moses, now the chief shepherd of Jethro's sheep, stood a little way away from the flock, his long shepherd's rod, or staff, in his hand. He was watching a strange sight. Not far from where he stood, a thorny bush of pale acacia flowers was glowing with a great, clear, shining flame. Yet not a twig was scorched, nor did any ashes fall to the ground. The bunches of blossom still lay delicately upon the spiked branches, fragrant and creamy-white, and the leaves made a pattern of golden green. How beautiful the flowers and foliage must have looked with the light of the mysterious flame glowing within the very heart of the little tree.

While Moses wondered, a voice came from the brightness and bade him take off his shoes, for he stood on holy ground. So Moses knew that he was in the presence of God.

Then the voice gave a message of comfort for the sad Israelites in Egypt, and told Moses of a land flowing with milk and honey, the country of Abraham, Isaac, and Jacob, who, God had promised, should be the fathers of a great nation. "They knew Me by another name," said the voice that spoke in the shining flame, "but, from now, they shall call me *I am that I am*. Go and bring their children to Me in this holy mountain, and tell them that Jehovah hath sent you to deliver them."

But Moses was afraid and said: "Behold, they will not hearken unto me."

The voice answered: "What is that in thine hand?"

Moses said: "A rod!"

Then the voice came clear again from the flame: "Cast it upon the ground!"

Moses obeyed, and, lo! the shepherd's staff turned into a serpent. Moses jumped out of its way in terror. But the voice said: "Put forth thine hand, and take it by the tail!"

When Moses did so, the twisting serpent changed back into a wand again. And God told him to take his brother Aaron to help him, and to go and show the miracle to the Israelites and to Pharaoh, and say that the Lord Jehovah claimed the people of Israel for His own.

So Moses set out for Egypt, with the staff of God in his hand.

One day soon after, the King of Egypt, seated on his throne in his splendid palace – a throne with golden serpents to ornament it – was told that two shepherds from the desert wished to speak to him; and he allowed them to be shown into his presence. They came in gravely; and one held a long rod, which Pharaoh thought was only the staff usually carried by a shepherd as he led his sheep. The King looked coldly and curiously at the two men, and inquired about their business.

Then one of them in low, grave tones rebuked Pharaoh for keeping the children of Israel in bondage. Then, in the name of the Lord Jehovah who had spoken from the holy mountain, he commanded Pharaoh to set the people free, that they might go and worship this great God in the wilderness.

Pharaoh stared at the two scornfully and said:

"Who is the Lord that I should obey His voice, to let Israel go? I know not the Lord, neither will I let Israel go!"

So Moses and his brother Aaron went silently away.

A second time, they came into Pharaoh's presence. Now it was Aaron who held the shepherd's rod quietly in his fingers. Once more, they demanded the freedom of the people of Israel in the name of Jehovah, the Lord God.

The monarch frowned angrily. Then, with a mocking laugh, he invited them to prove the might of their God by working a miracle. For the King did not believe that the two shepherds had any power in their hands at all.

Silently, Aaron lifted the long, slender staff, and flung it, straight and slim, at Pharaoh's feet. As it fell, it writhed and twisted in the air; the sun shone on it and showed it gleaming with scales. It dropped to the ground in the form of a live serpent, that lifted its head and hissed angrily at Pharaoh, and at the golden snakes that adorned his throne.

Pharaoh and his servants jumped back from the serpent, just as Moses had done beside the burning bush. But Pharaoh had at his court clever conjurers and magicians who could bring snakes out of empty bags and from corners of the royal rooms, in the same way that snake charmers do today. Pharaoh sent for the magicians, and they all turned their enchanters' wands into big snakes, that twisted and crawled, with Aaron's, upon the palace floor.

Then an astonishing thing happened. Aaron's serpent lifted its big flat head, opened its hissing mouth, and swallowed the magicians' serpents one by one. When Aaron lifted the great snake by the tail, it turned quietly into a rod again.

Still Pharaoh would not obey the message of God. So once more Moses and Aaron went out from the palace.

The next day, the proud Pharaoh went down to the river in the rosy dawn. Very likely he went there in order to worship the god of the river, in whom the Egyptians believed; morning after morning, he always made his way to the same spot. There, standing by the river's brink in the clear light of the risen sun, was the shepherd from the wilderness, with his brother Aaron, holding high the rod of God.

As Pharaoh came up to them, they stretched the rod over the river, where Pharaoh's god was believed to be all-powerful. They struck the waters with the rod in the sight of the King and all his servants. The sunlit ripples crimsoned, and the stream grew lurid and red. The rod of God had turned the waters of the river into blood.

Pharaoh and his servants stared at the crimson waters just as they had stared at the gleaming serpent. Then the King asked his magicians if they, too, could not turn water into blood. They showed him that they could, so again Pharaoh refused to believe in the power of the God of the Israelites.

Then Moses and Aaron, with their wonderful rod, brought up hundreds and hundreds of frogs from the river. The magicians of Pharaoh did the same. But Pharaoh now grew frightened, not only at what the shepherds could do, but also at the strange new powers of his own conjurers. He begged Moses to stop the frogs from coming out of the river in their thousands; Moses did so, and all the other frogs began to die. Then, when Pharaoh saw that no more frogs were coming, he forgot his fear, and said that, after all, he would *not* let the people of Israel go.

Then Aaron stretched out the rod again, and

When the lid was lifted, the baby began to cry (page 64)

Aaron's rod dropped to the ground in the form of a live
serpent (page 70)

struck it down upon the dust of the hot and sandy land. The dust became, as it were, alive with myriads of insects, so that the magicians, who could show no more enchantments, were as startled as Pharaoh himself.

Even then, Pharaoh would not believe. He grew sullen and angry, and still refused to let the people go. So, morning after morning, Moses and Aaron waited for him as he came down to the river to worship; morning after morning, one of them stretched out the rod and brought some strange and terrible thing to pass. At last, God said He would, Himself, pass over the land of Egypt about midnight and would strike with death the firstborn in every house that was not marked with the blood of lambs killed for the last supper that the Hebrews would ever eat in Egypt. The blood on the doorposts would tell God that His faithful people were within, and that they would not suffer the destroyer to enter. And, ever afterwards, they were, on a certain day, to observe the same Passover feast.

The Israelites did exactly as God told them and ate the Passover Lamb as they stood ready for their journey. God passed through the land as He had said. Then Pharaoh sent for Moses and Aaron in the very middle of the night, while all the Egyptians wept for their firstborn, and told them to hasten the Israelites away. "Get you forth," he cried, "go and serve the Lord as ye have said: Take your flocks and herds and be gone!"

All the men and women of the Egyptians echoed Pharaoh's cry and loaded the Israelites with gifts – jewels of silver, and jewels of gold, and fine clothing.

So the Israelites went away from the land of Goshen and set out across the desert of Shur. As they went, they saw always in front of them a pillar of cloud that streamed up from the earth to the sky. When night fell, a glow of redness showed in the high column of mist; as the darkness deepened, it became a pillar of fire. This was the sign of the Lord Jehovah, by which He showed them the way to go.

And so, men, women, and children, they set off for the Holy Mountain, that they might set up their tents and learn the teachings of the Great God among the dark rocks and the feathery tamarish shrubs and the scattered bushes of snow-white broom.

THE HOLY TENT IN
THE WILDERNESS

Moses did many more wonders with the staff of God as he led the people of Israel towards the Holy Mountain. You must read about all these things in the Bible – how, by the power of the wonderful rod, the Red Sea was divided so that the Israelites could travel through it; and how Pharaoh, who changed his mind and sent soldiers after them with horses and chariots, lost all his army in the waves. But the Israelites journeyed safely onwards and set up their tents all around about the foot of the mountain. Then God called to Moses from the shining cloud that hung over the very top. Moses went into the cloud and disappeared from the sight of the awed and wondering people below.

There, in the middle of the bright cloud, the Lord Jehovah told Moses to make a special tent for His beauty and His glory among the tents of the people themselves. Then, He could come down to them from the mountain, and be quite near them, and dwell with them. The children of Israel were to bring offerings for the Tent of God from the treasures that had been given to them by the Egyptians – gold and silver and brass; blue and purple and scarlet; fine linen and goats' hair; rams' skins dyed red, and fragrant wood; oil for the light; spices for anointing and for sweet incense; and precious stones for the High Priest to wear upon his breast.

God promised Moses that He would put great wisdom into the heart of a man called Bezaleel, of the tribe of Judah, to teach him how to turn all these offerings into beautiful things for the Tent of God. The scarlet and purple and blue were to be made into lovely curtains and hangings; the brass and silver into delicate ornaments; and the pure gold was, among other things, for a holy casket, with the Mercy-Seat above it, guarded by two bright angels stretching out their shining wings.

God also promised that He would come down and rest upon the golden Mercy-Seat between the wings of the bright angels, and teach Moses and the children of Israel the things He desired them to learn. So this beautiful casket, or the Ark, as it was called, was to be kept in a holy place within many-hued curtains, all embroidered with angels in scarlet and blue. In front of the last curtain, which hung in front of the Ark, they should place a golden candlestick, with seven branches made like almond-boughs in blossom, which would hold seven lamps of shining flame. The very shapes of the candlesticks were shown to Moses, as he stood in the glory of Jehovah's Mountain.

Then Bezaleel, and another Israelite called Aholiab, and every wise-hearted man and wise-hearted woman in the camp under the Holy Mountain, set to work to make the Tent of God. The wise-hearted women spun thread, and wove cloth, and did fine needlework, and gave their earrings and ornaments to Aholiab and Bezaleel. The wise-hearted men brought skins of badgers and goats, and hewed long planks of Shittim wood, which was the wood of the same kind of acacia tree from which Jehovah's voice had first spoken to Moses out of the flame. They all worked together for the glory and the beauty of the Tent of God.

When it was finished, Moses set the Tent up at the foot of the Holy Mountain, and all the people stood, watching. While they watched, a wonderful thing happened. The bright cloud on the mountain began to move slowly down the steep sides, over the white broom-bushes and the pretty acacia-flowers. It floated right up to where the Tent stood and then hung over it, shining more beautifully than ever. So

Moses and all the people knew that Jehovah had come down in the beautiful cloud to the lovely Tent that they had made for Him.

Three things were placed in the big golden casket that they called the Ark. First – the Tables of the Law, which were the Ten Commandments, printed in deep-cut letters upon two tablets of stone, and given by God to Moses for all the people to learn and to obey. The second was a little vase of manna. And to know what manna was, we must go back a little way to the time before God's wonderful Tent was finished.

You see, there were no fields of wheat or oats or barley around the foot of the Mountain where the camp of the children of Israel was spread. The people, who had lived so long in Egypt, did not know how to find food in the great wilderness that stretched around them. So they went, in anger, to Moses and told him that if he did not find food for them they would surely die. But Moses rebuked them for their lack of trust and said that, in the evening and the morning that were coming, they should see for themselves the loving kindness of God.

So, in the evening, when the purple dusk covered the desert with its mantle, and the sky flushed red in the west, the little brown quails of the wilderness came up and covered the camp; and the people killed and ate them. All through the night, the Mountain glowed with glory, as if some miracle were going to happen at the break of day. Down among the rocks, in the open spaces between the tents, the dew fell much more heavily than usual. And, when the people woke, they saw that all over the camp, the ground was quite silver with a thousand thousand beads of brightness.

They sparkled for a few minutes in the sunshine, and then they dried up with the warmth of the morning. But where the dew had lain, the people saw a lot of small round things covering the face of the wilderness and making the sand dunes quite white, as if the deep frosts of winter were upon them.

The people, wondering, asked each other what it could be that covered the face of the ground. And they said, "It is a gift! It is an unknown thing! 'Manna' must be its name."

But Moses, coming into the midst of them through the morning light, said: "This is the bread which the Lord hath given you to eat."

He told everybody, men and women and children, that they must gather the manna from the ground. So they brought out their jars and basins, and filled them with the wonderful new food. Then it was divided fairly among them. When the manna was made into cakes, it tasted like wafers mixed with honey.

So, morning after morning, during the years that they lived in the wilderness, the people of Israel gathered manna for their daily bread in the early coolness of the dawn. But, as soon as the noontime heats came, the white, mysterious food vanished like little flakes of snow. On the sixth morning of each week, the people gathered twice as much, for on the seventh day, the Sabbath, there was none.

It was in memory of this miraculous event that the vase of manna was put into the golden Ark with the Tables of the Law. And the third thing that was carefully laid there was Aaron's rod.

It was not the same holy staff that Moses and Aaron had carried into the presence of Pharaoh; it was freshly-cut, with eleven others, from the trees. For God told His people that, out of the twelve tribes of Israel, each of which was descended from one of Jacob's sons, He would choose a special family from whom the high priests for His service were to be taken. So the prince of each tribe was to give Moses a tree branch, on which the name of the tribe was written, in order that everybody might know to whom each tree branch belonged.

So Moses stood at the door of the Tent of God, and, one by one, the princes came and gave him their long, straight branches, clearly written with their names. Moses took the rods into the Tabernacle, passed through the embroidered curtains and stood before the shining Ark. And there he laid the rods of the twelve princes down.

So all night the rods lay in the Holy Place of God, and in the morning Moses went into the Tabernacle and brought them out.

As he held them up to the gaze of the twelve princes and their people, everybody saw that one of the tree branches had budded and brought forth green leaves and little tender blossoms, and had yielded almonds. It was the rod of Aaron, of the house of Levi, that had budded in the night, in answer to the whisper of God.

So Aaron and his sons were chosen high priests forever. As a token, the almond bough was laid in the golden Ark, with the little vase of manna and the stone Tablets of the Law.

The Ark was called "The Ark of the Covenant" because the Tablets, which, as you know, had the Ten Commandments written upon them, were a sort of promise, or covenant, between the Lord Jehovah and the people whom He had saved and blessed. If they kept His laws, then He, in return, would make them a great nation. So they were to follow Moses to a land where the goats gave as much sweet milk as anyone wanted, and where the wild bees made honey from the mountain flowers, the country where Abraham, Isaac, and Jacob had lived long, long ago.

But, before the Israelites could enter that country, they had many things to learn in the wilderness, for they often, by disobedience, showed themselves unworthy of their great destiny as the chosen people of God.

So, for forty years, they wandered to and fro in the wilderness. Boys grew to manhood, and young men became old men. In fact, scarcely any of those who had escaped from the bondage of Pharaoh lived to enter the Promised Land when their children did so. But wherever they stayed, the Holy Tent was always set up in their camps, and always, when they prayed to Jehovah, the beautiful cloud came down to the Mercy-Seat and shone between the golden angels of the Ark.

RUTH, THE DAUGHTER OF THE MOABITES

When the Children of Israel had learned to obey and follow the laws that Moses taught them, they were allowed to leave the wilderness and to go into Canaan, the Promised Land. It must have changed by then from the way it had been in the days of Jacob; for many great cities had been built by foreign kings on the mountains where once only the olive and fig trees had spread their branches and the small wild deer had played among the rocks. But it was always a fair and beautiful country; and, after long wars, the Children of Israel settled in the quiet valleys and built villages on the lower slopes of the hills. Moses was dead, but a great captain called Joshua led them and helped them to conquer the foreign kings. The people set up the beautiful Tent of Jehovah in a place called Shiloh, near the spot where Joseph had been sold to the Ishmaelites several hundred years before.

Bethlehem was one of the villages where the Children of Israel settled. After a time, there was a terrible famine there. No one had anything to eat, so many people left and went to settle in places where the harvests had been good. Among these people was a man called Elimelech, who went away with his wife, Naomi, and his two sons. They moved a long way from Bethlehem, beyond the wild, deserted salt lake that is called the Dead Sea, into the land of Moab, where the hills, in the distance, look red and strange. It was on one of these hills that Moses was buried, in a high, lonely grave. Elimelech settled there among the Moabites, and his two sons married two young Moabite girls, called Orpah and Ruth. But, before either of these young wives had any children, the sons of Naomi died. By now, Elimelech was dead also, so Naomi and her two daughters-in-law were left quite alone in the world.

Naomi longed for her own beautiful country of Canaan and did not want to die in the strange land of Moab. She heard, too, that the Lord had been merciful to Bethlehem again, and that, once more, the people had corn and wine and oil. So she left the place where she lived in Moab and set out for her old home. Orpah and Ruth went with her. But Naomi did not think that these daughters of the Moabites could be happy leaving their own people. So she begged them to turn back.

"Go," she said, "return each to your mother's house. And the Lord deal kindly with you, as ye have dealt with the dead, and with me! The Lord grant that ye may find rest, each of you, in the house of her husband!"

She kissed them tenderly, and they all wept at the thought of parting. Still Naomi urged the two others to turn back.

"Turn again, my daughters, go your ways!" she repeated, "I am an old woman. I only go to the land of my fathers to spend my last days among my own people!" And so, at last, kissing her mother-in-law and weeping, Orpah turned back.

But Ruth would not leave Naomi, nor let her continue her journey alone.

"Whither thou goest, I will go!" she said. "Where thou lodgest, I will lodge! Thy people shall be my people and thy God my God! Where thou diest I will die, and there will I be buried! The Lord do so to me, and more also, if ought but death part thee and me!"

When Naomi saw Ruth's steadfastness, she no longer tried to persuade her to turn back. And they came, like mother and daughter, to Bethlehem. There was, oh! such excitement in the little village as the people recognized Elimelech's wife. They said, "Is this Naomi?" But she answered sadly, "Nay, do not call me Naomi, but Mara, which means bitterness! For the Lord hath dealt very bitterly with me!"

Because, you see, except for sweet and faithful Ruth, Naomi had nobody near to her in the wide world, and, what grieved her most of all, no little grandchildren to carry on her husband's and her dead sons' name.

In this sad way, Naomi and Ruth came back to the plains and fields of Bethlehem, just when the people of the countryside were about to carry home the barley harvest. Among these folk were many kinsmen of Naomi's husband, and one of them, who was called Boaz, owned a great part of the land where the harvest was being gathered. Ruth asked Naomi if she might go and glean after the reapers. Gleaners are the poor women and children who, before machines did the work, used to go into the fields of the rich farmers, and, following behind the reapers, gather up the long stalks of wheat, or barley, or oats, that the men had dropped. In this way, Ruth thought that she could get a little food for Naomi and herself to eat.

So, when Naomi said, "Yes," Ruth went down the road to the barley fields, where the bearded, golden grain bent and rustled under the pure-blue, harvest skies. All around her were the reapers, cutting down the yellow stalks with their rounded, gleaming sickles, and binding them into long sheaves. It so happened that she went to a field belonging to Naomi's kinsman, Boaz, though she did not know it at the time. Presently Boaz came and stood among the busy workers and gave them greeting.

"The Lord be with you," said Boaz. And they answered, "The Lord bless thee."

Then Boaz saw Ruth, a little way off, wearing the dress of her native land of Moab, and he asked the reapers who she was. When they told him, he walked over the yellow barley stubble and spoke to her gently, telling her to go on gleaning in his field, for his servants would be kind to her and would give her water whenever she was thirsty. When she bent humbly before him and asked how it was he was so kind to a stranger, he told her that he had heard of her love and devotion to Naomi, and how she had come with her husband's mother into this land of strangers. "And," he added, "may the Lord recompense thy work, and a full reward be given thee of the Lord God of Israel, under whose wings thou art come to trust."

Ruth was greatly comforted by these kind words. When they all sat down to eat, Boaz called to her, even more kindly, to come and join them. And he gave her parched grain – roasted on a sieve – which was a popular food in Canaan, and she ate and was grateful. After dinner, Boaz told the reapers to let her glean quite close to them, among the very sheaves themselves, and to drop handfuls of good barley-ears as if by accident, so that she could pick them up.

The reapers did, and, when night fell, Ruth found that she had quite a lot of barley for Naomi and herself to grind and bake with oil to eat. Naomi, when she heard Ruth's story and saw her gleanings, said: "Blessed be the Lord, who hath not left off His kindness to the living and to the dead."

Now Naomi knew, by all the things Ruth told her, that the sweet young woman of the Moabites had, all at once, gained the love of Boaz, the kinsman of her dead husband. Naomi wanted Boaz to take Ruth to his heart and to make her his wife. But Boaz, who had indeed fallen deeply in love with Ruth, knew that Naomi had another kinsman, more closely related than himself, who had the first right to take the daughter-in-law Elimelech as his wife. So he said that this kinsman's consent must be obtained before he, Boaz, could prove to Ruth the love he felt for her.

So in the full sunshine of the morning, Boaz sat in an open place by the gate of the city. When the close

Ruth said to Naomi, "Whither thou goest, I will go"
(page 87)

The greatest gift that she could give was her son, Samuel
(page 98)

kinsman of whom he had spoken passed, he called to him and asked him to sit down also. Then he summoned ten elders – wise old men who were to be witnesses of what was to follow.

Boaz spoke to Naomi's kinsman and said, "Naomi, who was the wife of Elimelech, our brothers, has come back to Bethlehem from Moab and wishes to sell a piece of land that belonged to her husband in Bethlehem. It is for you to say, before anyone else, if you will buy it."

Naomi's kinsman answered, before all the elders: "I will buy it."

Then Boaz went on:

"The same day that you buy the field of Elimelech, you must also marry Ruth, the Moabitess, the wife of the dead, so that her children may inherit the land that belonged to her husband, Elimelech's son."

Naomi's kinsman shook his head: "That I cannot do!" he said. "I have little ones of my own to inherit all that belongs to me. I cannot share their inheritance with the children of a Moabitess. Therefore buy the field yourself."

So Boaz said to the elders and all the people who were listening: "Ye are witnesses this day that I have bought all that was Elimelech's and all that was his son's! And ye are witnesses, too, that I take Ruth,

Elimelech's son's wife, to be my wife. And her children and my children shall inherit all that was his."

So Boaz married sweet Ruth, and they had a little son. On the day that Naomi took the tiny baby into her arms, all the women who were her friends rejoiced with her. They said: "Blessed be the Lord that hath not left thee this day without a kinsman, whose name may be famous in Israel. And he – this baby – shall be to thee a restorer of thy life, to give sweetness to thine old age! For thy daughter-in-law, which loveth thee, which is better to thee than seven sons, hath borne him!"

The baby's name was called Obed. And his son, when he grew up, was Jesse, the father of David the shepherd, who, as we shall see, became King over all Israel.

SAMUEL, THE CHILD IN THE HOUSE OF GOD

he Holy Tent that Moses had made in the wilderness was, you remember, set up in a place called Shiloh. From the door of the Tent, Joshua had taught and guided the people, just as Moses had done.

Then Joshua died, too. In those days, there was no king in Israel. Instead, everyone did what seemed right to himself, without thinking of other people. So there was a great deal of fighting and trouble among the tribes.

All the time the House of God stood on the little hill of Shiloh, where great oaks grew wide and free, dropping their acorns upon the grass. In the oaks, the turtledoves built their nests of sticks and cooed softly over the pure white eggs. Big jays made harsh noises, and black and white magpies chattered back to the jays. There were black storks with homes in the firs, and common storks on the house roofs, and fields of flax, where the flowers were as blue as the cloudless sky. Here was the very well where Jacob's sons had once fed and watered their flocks, and you could still see shepherd boys taking care of the sheep and lambs. But there were vineyards now, also, where the big leaves grew green, and grapes hung in purple bunches from the brown stems. Little towers were set in the middle of these vineyards; and watchmen, in warm sheepskin coats, kept guard over the fruit all night. Great gnarled fig trees yielded green and purple figs; and the silver olive branches trembled and shimmered in the sun. The houses of the villages were built, very often, of bricks and had wide, flat roofs, where the women spread out the soaked stalks of flax to dry into thread for linen. Life was altogether different now from the way it had been among the tents of the shepherd-princes, long ago.

The Holy Tent on the little hill was circled with houses of the priests, but the shining cloud never came to hang over it now, for many of the people had forgotten God and worshipped the idols of the foreign kings. The curtains of blue and crimson and purple were faded and worn, for, since the wise-hearted women had spun and woven them in the desert, several hundred years had passed. The lamps of the golden candlesticks made like almond branches were often allowed to go out. Where the people had once sung praises, there was now only the singing of the birds.

An old man called Eli acted as High Priest; but he was tired and sad, and unable to stop the wickedness of the people. And Eli's sons were the most wicked of all. So it seemed as if Israel were lost to goodness forever. And then, one day, the presence of the Lord returned to the forsaken Tent at Shiloh. And it came back in answer to the loving worship of a little child.

Some of the people of Israel, you see, still remembered the God who had brought them out of Egypt, and they came to Shiloh, once every year to offer gifts to Jehovah, as Moses had taught them – barley and figs and olives, and sometimes goats or lambs. Among these yearly pilgrims were a man and his wife from Mount Ephraim, on the other side of the valley. One day, as Eli, the old High Priest, sat in a seat by the post of the Tent, he saw this woman, who was kneeling at the door of the House of God, weeping bitterly. Her lips were moving all the time, as if she talked to herself. After watching her for a little, Eli asked what she was doing.

Then the woman poured out her trouble to the old Priest. She had been praying for a child, because she had no little ones to make her happy. She told Eli that, if God would only grant her a son, she would give the child to the Lord to serve in the Holy Tabernacle all his life.

Something of the old spirit of power and grace filled Eli's heart. And he said:

"Go in peace! And the God of Israel grant thy petition that thou hast asked of Him!"

So the woman, who was named Hannah, went away, hopeful and rejoicing.

Well, after some time, her prayer was answered, and Eli's blessing was fulfilled. A dear little boy was born to Hannah and her husband in their home on Mount Ephraim. The mother, in her joy, called the baby "Samuel" because she said, "That means 'Asked of God.' "

The next year, Hannah's husband went to Shiloh, as usual, to worship, and to carry his offerings to the Lord. But Hannah would not go with him.

"No!" she said. "The next time I go I will take my dear little son Samuel with me! I will show him to the Lord in the Tabernacle! And then I will leave him, that he may stay there and serve God forever!"

Samuel's father, who loved Hannah better than anybody in the world, told her to do as seemed good to her and to keep her promise to the Lord.

Then, when Samuel was a little older, just able to run about and play with the other children, Hannah took gifts of cattle from her husband's herds, and flour from the silo, and a bottle of wine made from the sweet vineyard grapes, and went to Shiloh. And she took little Samuel with her.

So Eli, one day, saw again the woman who had prayed at the door of the Holy Tent. This time, she was bringing many gifts for the Lord Jehovah. And the greatest gift of all was her tiny son.

In rapt and earnest words, she told Eli who she was. "Oh, my Lord!" said she, "I am the woman that stood by thee here, praying unto the Lord! For this child I prayed! And the Lord has answered my prayer! Therefore, as long as he lived shall he be lent to the Lord!"

Eli looked down at the little innocent child. Samuel gazed up into the old Priest's face with earnest, surprised eyes. Then Hannah told her little son always to be good and to worship God, and she left him in the Holy Tent, with the old Priest, forever.

I do not think little Samuel was lonely. He lived among such interesting things, and he must have liked to look at the beautiful angels so cleverly embroidered upon the fine old curtains, and at the golden almond boughs of the great candlestick. He learned to mix the spices for the incense – the holy perfume that was burned on certain days – and you can imagine how he would enjoy pounding the fragrant stuff "very small" as Moses had commanded, and putting it to burn in the censer, which was a beautiful vase of gold. Then he would pour the glistening yellow oil into the lamps, set a light to the floating wicks, and watch the flame shine among the shadows till all was bright and clear.

He wore a small linen ephod, which hung from his shoulders as if it were a tiny gown. And his mother, every year, when she came to Shiloh to worship, brought him a little coat that she had made for him. What a great day that must have been for Hannah and Samuel! How they would try on the coat together, and see, by its size, how much Samuel had grown. And he would, I am sure, tell his mother of the beauties of the inner parts of the Holy Tent, and describe to her the angels, and the lamps, and the golden bells on the hem of the High Priest's robe. Then he would kiss her goodbye and wave his hand to her as she went down the mountain path into the dusk of the valley on her way home.

So Samuel lived – a little, sweet, pure-hearted child – among the lovely worn embroideries and old mysterious treasures of the Holy Tent, passing busily through them in the daytime and sleeping in their very midst at night. And the Lord saw him there and loved him, and chose him for His own.

One night, then, Samuel lay down to sleep in the quiet shadows of the curtains, where the lamps of God were burning with a soft light, before dying away into darkness. Eli, the old High Priest, kept watch near at hand. But Eli's eyes grew heavy and dim with drowsiness, and presently his tired lids closed. And then Samuel, lying quiet and dreamy on his mattress, heard a voice in the Tent of God.

"Samuel!" called the voice, "Samuel!"

"Here am I!" answered little Samuel quickly, starting up. And he pattered across on his bare feet to Eli, for he thought that the Priest had called.

But Eli said, "I called not! Lie down again!" So little Samuel went back to his mattress and lay down again.

Then, a second time, came the voice: "Samuel!"

Again Samuel jumped up and ran to Eli. "Here am I!" said the child earnestly. "For thou *didst* call me."

But still Eli said that the little boy was mistaken. "I called not, my son! Lie down again!"

So, once more, Samuel went back and lay down. And the Tent was very still, with only the sound of the night breeze rustling in the oaks outside.

Then, a third time, the silence was broken. The urgent voice rang out again: "Samuel!"

Then at last Eli, when Samuel came once more to him, knew that the Lord had called the child. And he said, "Go; lie down! And if the voice comes again, say, 'Speak, Lord; for Thy servant heareth!' "

So Samuel lay down for the third time and listened breathlessly. And the voice came to him once more, straight out of the Holy Place where the Ark stood behind the curtains.

"Samuel!"

Then Samuel, trembling, yet full of joy, whispered:

"Speak, for Thy servant heareth!"

And, in the quietness of the night, the Lord Jehovah told the child that great changes were to take place in Israel, and that those who did wrong were to make way for those who did right. Samuel listened earnestly to all that the Lord said to him. Then the voice died away, and, until the dawn came, all was quiet in the House of God.

In the morning, the child got up and opened the doors wide, as usual, and breathed the fresh sweet air. But the voice was clear in his memory. Only, as Eli's sons were those who did the worst wrong, he was afraid to answer the Priest's questions. But when, at last, he did so, Eli said with earnest faith:

"It is the Lord! Let Him do what seemeth good to Him!"

And, after that night, the Lord appeared again in Shiloh, so perhaps the people in the valley could sometimes see the beautiful cloud shining again over the Holy Tent, and would know that the Lord Jehovah was teaching Samuel, just as He had taught Moses in the Wilderness, long ago.

THE ARK
OF THE LORD

One morning, in Canaan, the sun rose upon a rather terrible sight. Two long wide camps of war-tents were spread over the grassy plains where usually the sheep and goats grazed so peacefully. From the tents came the clash of arms and the hum of great crowds of soldiers. The Israelites and the Philistines were about to fight a big battle.

The Philistines were a nation of sea-robbers, pirates who lived on the coast of Canaan. Their palaces and temples overlooked the golden shores and violet-blue waters of the Great Sea – the sea we now call the Mediterranean. And the chief god that they prayed to was a Fish-God. A very strong and powerful people they were! They had five Kings who moved from place to place in iron chariots, and it was always a time of awe for the Israelites when they heard the rolling wheels of the sea-robbers' carriages and the thudding gallop of their war horses, coming through the lonely hill passes and across the quiet meadows. This time, though, the children of Israel were ready for battle, because Samuel, now a grave and beautiful youth about twenty years old, had told them that they would have to fight the Philistines very soon. And, as all the people knew, Samuel was taught by God Himself.

So, when the sun was fully risen and the world was flooded with a light too lovely for a scene so terrible, the armies met each other with the deep-toned chantings and sullen clang of a mighty old-world battle. And the Philistines won the day. When night fell on the exhausted and heartbroken Israelites, they met together in their camp and wept over their dead. Then the old men among them said:

"Let us send to Shiloh for the Ark of Jehovah! Surely that will save us, as it used to do!"

For, in the old days, Joshua, when he fought the foreign armies, had always made the priests carry the Ark in front of the Israelites; just as, in later wars, the soldiers would carry the banner of the king.

So messengers went through the dark, starry night to Shiloh and brought the Ark of God secretly to the field of battle. And, when the Children of Israel saw the Ark carried into the midst of their tents they gave the old ringing, well-known battle cry — that battle cry that used always to burst out so triumphantly when they knew that Jehovah was in their midst.

The Philistines heard the mighty shout and asked what it meant. The word ran through their ranks that the Ark of the Israelites' God had been brought into the enemy's camp. They were frightened, and said to each other:

"The shepherd-people have brought out the Ark of their wonderful God, who did such terrible things to the Egyptians! Let us escape!"

Then their captains turned on them angrily and commanded them be men – not frightened servants of the Hebrews. So they took courage again and lined up in front of their tents, ready, once more, for battle.

There, in the morning light, stood the shining golden casket, with the beautiful carved angels that Bezaleel had made. Behind it waited the rows of Israelite soldiers – breathless, silent, watching for the sea-robbers to take instant flight. But the Israelites had neglected the great Jehovah of Battles too long. After the first moment of awed hesitation, the worshippers of the Fish-God rushed forward upon their enemies, killing them in hundreds and driving them in full flight over the plain to take refuge in their tents. Then the Philistines took the holy Ark of the Covenant and carried it away to their own country on the shores of the Great Sea.

When they reached the coast, the five Kings had the Ark taken into the temple of the Fish-God. It was set up by the side of their own big silver and wooden image, which had the head and hands of a man, and the scaly tail of a fish.

What a strange sight it must have been in that dim temple! On stormy nights, the winds of the Great Sea howled across the few miles of low shore right up to the gates of the city of Ashdod, where the Fish-God's temple stood. These winds from the west would bring the smell of the salt weeds into the temple; so that the Fish-God must have seemed like a monster merman in a darkling cave, when the five Kings, and the priests, and the magicians, after offering incense to their idol, went away into the twilight and left the Ark of Jehovah behind.

Did they wonder what would happen? Did they think that perhaps, in the morning, the image of the Fish-God would glow with some new mysterious life and strength and power? The Bible does not tell. But what it does tell is that, when they returned in the early dawn, they found Dagon, the Fish-God, knocked down to the very earth, lying stretched out on the ground in the temple, in front of the Ark.

The priests set the idol up again, awed and wondering. But, the next night, the Fish-God had fallen a second time. And, this second time, its head and its hands were cut away from it, and only its fishy stump remained.

After that, the people of Ashdod were all seized with sickness, so they sent the Ark of God away to Gath, another city of the five sea-robber Kings. Then illness fell, too, upon the people of Gath. So the Kings sent the Ark to Ekron, a third city that belonged to them. But the people of Ekron would not have it. And, at last, after seven months, the Kings called together all the priests of the Fish-God and begged to know what was the best thing to do with the Ark of the God of Israel.

The priests of the Fish-God told the five Kings to have a new cart made, and to take two milking cows that had never yet been yoked, and to harness them to the cart. Then, said the priests, the two little calves that always ran by the side of their mothers must be taken to their home meadows. The Ark of God must be laid upon the cart, with jewels of gold in a coffer, or box, by its side. The cows must be set free to take whatever path they chose. If they drew the Ark to Bethshemesh, which lay at the foot of the hills that divided the land of the shepherd-people from the land of the sea-robbers, the Kings would understand that it was the Israelites' God who had smitten the

David, the shepherd boy, played sweet music on his harp
(page 115)

David leaped upon the giant's prostrate form (page 123)

people of Ashdod, of Gath, and of Ekron. But if the mother cows went back to their baby calves, it would be a sign that the sickness and the trouble had come only by chance.

The Kings did as the priests commanded. In their iron chariots, they sat as their servants, under the orders of the priests, harnessed the cows to the new wooden cart, set the Ark of God upon it, and laid the jewels of gold by the side. Then the cows were set free. Instead of turning homewards to the meadows where their little calves nibbled at the grass, they hastened right away towards the hills of Bethshemesh, lowing as they went, and pulling the cart behind them.

Then the five Kings of the fish-robbers gave rein to their horses and followed behind. Can you picture that strange and beautiful procession across the green pastures to the distant, hazy hills? How the sun would shine on the golden Ark, and the bright jewels, and the sleek, smooth coats of the cows! And how the five Kings, wondering, awed, expectant, would rein in their big, high-stepping horses, and follow in the track of the cattle! On and on they went, until Bethshemesh was in sight. The Israelites, reaping their wheat harvest in the valley, heard the lowing of the cows, and the rolling of the wheels, and the sound of the horses' hoofs. And, looking up, they saw that, in this wondrous fashion, the Ark of God was being returned to them.

Straight to a tall pillar that stood in a field went the two cows. There they paused. Then the priests came and took the Ark of Jehovah from the cart. The five Kings, in deep wonderment, turned and drove back again to Ekron.

But the men of Bethshemesh were curious and looked into the Ark, and the Lord slew many of them. So they begged the men of Kirjathjearim to take it away. The men of Kirjathjearim carried it to the house of a good man who lived on the quiet slopes of the hills. And in this house, among the mountain trees, the beautiful casket made of gold stayed for twenty years.

DAVID
AND GOLIATH

One day, an old man with white hair, bowed shoulders, and tired, sad eyes, stood on the hillside above Bethlehem, looking down into the valley below. In his withered hands, he held a horn, like the drinking cups that were used in the olden days; a mantle lay upon his stooping shoulders. The horn was filled with oil, which smelled wonderfully sweet, and he was holding it very carefully. Bees were humming in the sweet flowering myrtles that grew nearby; far behind, in the distance, rose the purple heights of Mount Moriah. Sheep browsed among the flowers below, and green barley was sprouting in the fields of Boaz and Ruth. Above all the other sounds of the valley – the bleats of the little lambs and the voices of young children – came the rippling sweetness of a shepherd boy's harp.

The old man was Samuel, now a great prophet in Israel, who had chosen a King for the people – a fine, strong youth called Saul. For some years, Saul's rule had been good, but now he was doing many wrong things. So God had told Samuel that He had chosen another King, whom Samuel was to anoint with the oil that he carried so carefully in the horn. This new King was one of the sons of Jesse, the Bethlehemite, the grandson of Boaz and Ruth.

So Samuel, sad at heart because of Saul's failure, went down to the village of Bethlehem, and called Jesse and his sons to come and make a sacrifice before God. They came, with all the elders and other people of the village, and Samuel stood by the place of sacrifice with the horn of oil in his hand.

Then, in obedience to what Samuel told him, Jesse made his sons pass before the prophet one by one. Eliab, a tall handsome man, came first. And Samuel, remembering that Saul had been chosen for his strength and beauty, said to himself, "Surely this is the chosen King!" But he heard the voice of God whisper:

"Look not on his face, nor at his height and strength! He is not My chosen one! Man looketh upon the eyes, but the Lord looketh into the heart!"

Then Jesse called his second son, who was also big and fine, and made him pass before Samuel. But Samuel shook his head, and said:

"Neither hath the Lord chosen this man!"

So, one by one, the seven sons stood before Samuel,

and then passed on. And Samuel said to Jesse:

"The Lord hath not chosen these! Are these *all* thy children?"

Jesse answered in surprise: "There is only the youngest left. And he is a mere shepherd boy, out in the pastures with the sheep."

But Samuel commanded Jesse to send for the shepherd boy and told everybody to wait until he came.

So messengers were sent for Jesse's youngest son, and, by and by, up to the quiet place of sacrifice, breaking the silence among the little group of waiting men, floated the trembling music of a harp. Then, playing his pretty tunes and walking with a springing step along the hilly path that led from the pastures, came David, the shepherd boy, into the midst of them.

Such a fine, fair lad he was, with bright eyes, rosy cheeks, and slim, active limbs. His little sheepskin coat lay on his shoulders, and his harp was in his hands. All eager and curious he came; and Samuel, the moment he saw him, heard the whisper of God:

"Arise! Anoint him! For this is he!"

So, in the presence of the seven brothers, and of their father Jesse, the old priest went to meet the shepherd lad. He raised the horn of oil and anointed

David. And the perfume of myrrh and aloe and cassia flowed over the boy's garments as David, wide-eyed and wondering, let Samuel touch his hair, and his lips, and his fingers with the fragrant golden liquid. Then the spirit of God came upon David. Awed, yet happy, he went back again to his sheep.

There he stayed in the pasture, day after day, watching the flocks, and keeping them in place by means of stones from his slingshot. If a sheep strayed too far from the others, David would fit a big round stone into the sling and carefully fling the pebble right in front of the wandering ewe or lamb. When the stone landed in front of it, knocking up little bits of grass and earth, the sheep, though quite unhurt, would be frightened, and would turn to run back to the flock. In this way, the shepherd boy grew very skilled with his stones and his sling. Always, morning and evening, he led the sheep with the music of his harp.

Most of the shepherd boys in Canaan could play on little flute pipes; the flocks knew the sound and would come to the music. But David, with his harp, made lovelier melodies than all the rest. So, when he led his sheep either to the pastures or to the fold, the sweetest tunes would echo over the quiet valleys and chalky slopes of the hills. The people who heard the music as they went home at night after cutting their grain, or winnowing their barley, would know that David, the shepherd boy, walked near them in the twilight, playing his harp.

Sometimes he had to take his sheep and goats into lonely places where wild beasts lived in caves among the rocks. One night, a lion came out of these caves, with a bear close behind. The lion went stealthily into the middle of the flock and snatched a little goat kid in its cruel mouth. The bear would have done the same, but brave young David rushed up to the lion and seized the kid. Then he caught the great beast by its beard, struck it, and slew it as it struggled. He did the same to the bear; and so, through his skill and bravery, the sheep and kids and lambs were saved.

And all the time that David led his sheep among the green pastures and beside the still waters, where they could feed peacefully and drink as they pleased, he was the anointed King of Israel, who was, one day, to reign over the whole land.

So the weeks passed, and David's mind was always quiet and happy and full of peace, because, as you know, the Spirit of God had come upon him. But every bit of King Saul's ease of heart was gone; from him, the Spirit of God had departed. Evil thoughts tormented him, and troubled fancies filled his brain.

His servants said that an evil demon had been sent into the King.

Then they went to Saul and told him of their fears for him. "Behold, O lord the King!" they said. "An evil spirit from God troubleth thee! So let us, thy servants, seek out someone who plays sweetly upon the harp, that, by his music, thou may be made well."

When Saul consented, they told him that the young son of Jesse, the Bethlehemite, was fair to look at, brave and strong. And, they added, he could play very beautifully upon the harp. For everybody in the surrounding countryside knew the sound of David's music and found something strangely beautiful in its notes.

So King Saul sent messages to Jesse, saying: "Send thy son, David the shepherd boy, to me!"

You may imagine how surprised Jesse was to receive such a message, and how he wondered what it meant. He called David from the pastures and told him he was to go to the royal house, for Saul had sent for him. And he loaded a donkey with presents for Saul – fine white bread and sweet red wine. He sent the King a little goat kid as well. So, taking all these gifts, David set out to obey the summons of the King.

When Saul saw David, with his bright eyes and

rosy cheeks and quick springing footsteps, he felt a great love for the shepherd boy spring up in his heart. He took David into his service and made him his arms-bearer.

Then, when the evil spirit came to the King and tormented him so that he was worn out with sad and troubled thoughts, he would tell David to play on the harp. Then, all through the royal rooms, the sweet music sounded, just as it had floated across the Bethlehem valleys and hills. Perhaps David sang sometimes as well – perhaps his lips formed the very psalms that he wrote when he was older. Who knows? He may have hushed Saul's sorrow with the words, "The Lord is my Shepherd, I shall not want. He maketh me to lie down in green pastures; He leadeth me beside the still waters; He restoreth my soul!" For we know that the Spirit of God was in David, and when he played, Saul was refreshed and made well and filled with all his old content.

But the monarch, listening to David's tunes, never guessed that the shepherd boy had been anointed King of Israel in his own stead!

Soon afterwards, when David had gone back to his sheep, the sea-robbers once again came across the border, bringing a great army to overthrow Saul's kingdom. Among them was a mighty champion, a giant called Goliath, who wore a curious brass helmet and an enormous coat of mail. He had brass from his knees to his feet and a brass breastplate, and he carried a huge spear and a sword as well. And his shield-bearer went before him.

He stood out, morning and evening, for everybody to see, in front of the glittering ranks of the sea-robbers, and he called to the armies of Israel, opposite, crying:

"Choose a man of yourselves, O Israelites, who will come, single-handed, and fight with me! If he can kill me, then we will be your servants. But if I kill him, then you and your armies shall be subject to us for evermore!"

All the people of Israel looked at the great giant, in his strong glittering battledress. Not one of them dared to go out, single-handed, to give Goliath battle.

So morning and evening, for forty days, the Philistine giant sent his proud cry ringing across the space between the two armies. David's three eldest brothers were among the Israelite soldiers; but, although they were tall and strong, each was afraid to go out alone and fight the giant.

Then, one day, the shepherd boy came to visit them from his father's pastures, bringing them and their captain gifts of cheeses and barley bread.

As David stood talking to his brothers, the proud cry came, as usual, ringing across from the Philistines' camp:

"Choose a man of yourselves, O Israelites, who will come single-handed and fight with me!"

David, looking up, saw, standing out from among the ranks of the enemy, the great, haughty, fully-armed giant!

The shepherd boy gazed first at the giant and then at his brothers and their companions. He was amazed because nobody was brave enough to answer the proud and defiant call. But when he asked why that was, his brothers were angry with him and said he had only left home that he might see a battle. So David asked everybody the reason why no one went out and killed Goliath. At last, Saul himself heard of the young shepherd boy who was so surprised at his soldiers' want of courage.

Saul sent for David, but he did not recognize his former harp player at all. He asked many questions, and the shepherd youth said quite simply, in reply, that as nobody else would go, he was prepared to fight Goliath himself.

Everybody, including Saul, shook their heads, and they half-smiled, and said: "Goliath is a great giant, trained to be a soldier! You are only a stripling! He would kill you, instead of you killing him!"

But brave young David persisted. At last Saul, looking at him admiringly though anxiously, said:

"Go, then! And the Lord be with you!"

So the King told his arms-bearer to put his own royal coat of mail upon David and to give him his breastplate, his helmet, and his spear. But when David tried them on, they were too large and too heavy for him. He took them off and said that he could not wear them.

Then the shepherd boy, in his simple shepherd's smock, went down to the brook in the valley, chose five big smooth stones and put them into the bag in which he usually carried his food. With his sling in one hand and his shepherd's staff in the other, he went out in front of both armies and stood where the great giant could see him.

Then Goliath came marching across the open space, with his shield-bearer in front. He looked in angry scorn at the fair-headed, bright-cheeked lad with the sling and the staff.

"You come out with a stick as if you meant to beat a dog!" cried the contemptuous giant. "Come a little nearer, and I will give your dead body to the birds of the air and the wild beasts of the field!"

But David answered steadily: "I come to you, not in my strength, but in the name of the Lord God of all armies!"

Then, all at once, he darted forward, fitting a stone into his sling as he ran. Just before he came within reach of the giant's spear, he slung the stone with his old, well-known, fast movement, and the stone struck the great Philistine on the forehead, above his eyes.

Goliath fell forward, and lay unconscious upon the ground, his brass helmet pressing down and hiding the deep wound. Then David leaped upon the prostrate form and, seizing the giant's own sword, drew it from the sheath and cut off Goliath's head. And the whole army of the Philistines, when they saw that their great champion was dead, turned and fled.

The Israelites, with great shouts, pursued them. But David was led before King Saul, carrying Goliath's head in his hand.

Then Saul, in a bewildered manner, gazed at the lad, and seemed to recall his face. Looking from David's frank, brave countenance to the bleeding head of the terrible giant, he said confusedly: "Whose son art thou, young man?"

And David, quite simply, answered, "I am the son of thy servant, Jesse the Bethlehemite."

In this way, Saul knew that the lad who had slain

the mighty Philistine giant was the youth who had once been his arms-bearer, and who had driven the spirit of misery from him with the sweet music of his harp.

David lived for a long time with Saul and his son Jonathan, and, he became King of Israel himself.

When he was King, he took the Holy Tent of God to Jerusalem and set it up there. Solomon, his son, made a beautiful Temple for the Golden Ark, which you must read about in the Bible, for it would take pages and pages to describe. In addition to the Temple, Solomon built a palace of cedar wood and sat to pass judgment on an ivory throne, with carved lions on each side of the steps that led to it. In the gardens were peacocks, and strange monkeys clambered among the trees. His stables were full of horses, and his chariots were most magnificent, and kings and queens came to see his glory. He was wise and good, yet he never loved the Lord as faithfully as did his father, who had once been a shepherd boy of Bethlehem, leading his sheep to pasture with the music of his harp.

NEITHER RAIN
NOR DEW

an you picture to yourself a beautiful palace of ivory? And can you imagine it set among pink almond blossoms, and evergreen laurels, and old gnarled fig trees, while the grassy slopes around it are filled with the singing of nearly a hundred brooks?

Such was the house of Ahab, King of Samaria, which he had built in the royal city begun by his father, King Omri, among the beautiful meadows of Shechem, where little Joseph had once wandered in search of his brothers and their flocks of sheep. Not very far away was Joseph's grave, for the Children of Israel had brought back the body of their great forefather almost to the very spot where the Ishmaelites had bought him and taken him away to Egypt.

A spreading oak close by was Jacob's oak, and under its branches stood a tall pillar of stone. Every child who passed by the pillar knew that it had been set up there by Joshua, and that, before he had raised it, he had gathered the Israelites together to remind them of their old, old promise to worship Jehovah. "This stone has heard your words," he had said. "It shall always stand under the oak in witness." So there it stood, with the Holy Tent not very far above it.

Ahab, living in his ivory palace, ruled over ten tribes of Israel – ten tribes who had rebelled against the royal family of David at Jerusalem. But Ahab cared nothing for the grave, or the sweet memories of the shepherd-princes, of whom the people in the valley below told so many stories. The King of Samaria had married a wife from among the heathen rulers, a princess called Jezebel, who did not believe in the God of Isaac and Jacob, but worshipped only the sun and the moon.

Persuaded by Jezebel, Ahab made a great temple on the hill, to glorify "Baal." The word Baal means "master" or "power" – and Jezebel believed that all the power of life fell to earth from the sky in the rays of the sun and the moon. So, within Baal's temple were set up strange idols made of ebony. A great poet, Jeremiah, described these idols long afterwards and said that they were as upright as palm trees, and robed in crimson and purple, and decked with silver and gold. Chains and nails held them in their places, and they were carried on men's shoulders, because by themselves they could neither come nor go. Four

The ravens brought bread and meat to Elijah every day
(page 131)

Elisha pressed the child close, and he opened his eyes
(page 139)

hundred and fifty priests were put into the temple, to hold services dedicated to these enormous statues, carved and decorated by the hands and tools of men. How different from the old pure worship of the true God, who had told the Israelites that they must never bow down to a "graven image," nor the likeness of anything on earth, or in the sky or sea.

Every day, then, Ahab and Jezebel and their household went in procession to the big temple, and prayed to the image of the sun-god, or the statue of the goddess of the moon. Then Ahab was escorted by servants to his ivory porch, where he sat on a throne and settled matters that were brought before him by his people. One morning, as he was giving his judgments, a stranger, wrapped in a mantle, mounted the steps that led up to the entrance of the porch. Ahab, from his fine throne, watched the stranger come. He could wonder very much who it could be, for the people of the desert were not ruled by the Kings of Samaria. He waited, however, to hear his servants proclaim the stranger's name.

The servants spoke to the man in the mantle, and then they announced him:

"Elijah, the Tishbite, who has come here from Gilead, asks audience of the King!"

Ahab looked inquiringly at the newcomer, and

everybody else stood listening. Then Elijah raised his arm before the King and pointed to the temple where the people prayed to the sun and the moon.

"As the Lord God of Israel liveth," he cried in a loud voice, "the God before whom I stand! There shall be neither dew nor rain in the land until the Lord sends it once more in answer to my prayer!"

Then, before the King and the courtiers had recovered from their amazement, he turned away and went down the hill again to the plains. And Ahab was left to his worship of the statues of the sun-god and the goddess of the moon.

From that day, all the moisture in the land began to dry up. No soft, warm rain fell from the sky in the daytime, and, worse still, no silvery dew spangled the grass at night. All the little bubbling streams that flowed by the ivory palace disappeared from their pebbly beds. Hot and cruel, like a great ball of brass, the sun stared down on the scorched meadows where Joseph's young feet had trodden among the flowers; cold and cruel, and without any softness, the moon glittered through the fading leaves of Jacob's oak.

Ahab and Jezebel, who thought that Elijah had done all this, searched throughout the whole land to find him. Jezebel wanted to put him to death with the other prophets. Except Obadiah, the governor, hid a hundred of these prophets, for he knew that there was a God who was far above the sun and the moon.

And where was Elijah all this time?

He was hidden in a cave beside the rushing, leaping waters of the brook Cherith. Great rocks overhung the gorge through which the stream ran, and black ravens nested among the crags. And the ravens, commanded by God, every morning and every evening brought bread and meat to Elijah, while, to quench his thirst, he drank the cold water from the stream.

By and by, because there was still no rain in the land, even the deep churning brook of Cherith dried up, and Elijah was taken care of, for a time, by a widow. She had only a little food left in the house when he went to her. But, so long as he lived there, the food, by a miracle, never grew less.

Then the time came when God told Elijah to go to Ahab again.

Ahab, when he saw the prophet, was afraid, but he dared not do anything to him now. Everyone in his kingdom was dying of famine under the sun and moon, for, without rain and dew, nothing would grow. The King asked Elijah if it were he that was troubling Israel. But Elijah told Ahab that the trouble had come through himself.

Then the four hundred and fifty priests of the sun-god went, with Elijah and Ahab, to Mount Carmel, a mountain with rugged slopes and deep gorges from the top of which they could see the sea. The priests of the sun and moon gods laid their sacrifice upon an altar. All day, they cried to their idols to send fire down onto the altar. But no fire came. Then towards evening, Elijah built an altar of twelve stones and had a great trench dug all around it. He made the people fill the trench with water from a strange deep well on the top of Mount Carmel. Then he put his sacrifice upon the altar and cried out to the great God whom Ahab had forgotten. And the fire of the Lord fell upon Elijah's altar, and it burned the sacrifice and shone in triumphant glory on the awed face of Ahab, and the frightened countenances of the sun-god priests, and the grave glad eyes of Elijah. The brightness sent shadows flickering among the dying trees, so that to those who watched in the hot parched valley below it must have seemed a beacon light of hope and joy.

Then Elijah had the four hundred and fifty priests taken down into the valley and put to death. And Elijah told Ahab that the fire that had fallen from heaven was a promise from the Most High God that He would no longer leave the land to the mercy of the false idols, but would send His refreshing dews to it once more.

"Arise, eat and drink!" said Elijah to Ahab, "for there is a sound of abundance of rain."

So Ahab was comforted, and Elijah went back to the top of Mount Carmel with his servant and began to pray. He said to the servant, "Go, and look towards the sea!" The servant went, and came back, saying, "There is nothing." Seven times, Elijah told him to go. And the seventh time the servant returned, and cried: "Behold! There ariseth out of the sea a little cloud, like a man's hand!"

Then Elijah bade him hurry down to Ahab in the valley and say that the storm was coming. Almost immediately, the clouds rushed up black and strong. The winds blew, and the heavens seemed to open. Down upon the parched, weary, thirsty earth, left so long to the burning sun and the cold white moon alone, fell the silver torrents of merciful rain. Ahab sprang into his chariot and fled home before the valley was quite flooded; while Elijah, the swift-footed man of the desert, ran ahead of him, fleeter and stronger than ever the horses of the King.

ELISHA AND THE MANTLE OF ELIJAH

he sun was beating down on the plains one day as a long train of oxen, yoked two and two, were working in a wide-stretching field. Each team was guided by a man in a loose blue cotton robe, with a white cloth wound around his head. Elijah stood on the edge of the field and watched the oxen and their drivers pass.

Slowly the long train moved on. As the last driver came near to the prophet, Elijah took off his mantle and laid it upon the man's shoulders. The man at once left his oxen and his furrower. He went and said farewell to his people, and he followed Elijah until the day that God took the great prophet to Himself.

The man's name was Elisha, and week after week he went with Elijah, as the prophet went from place to place. Then one day, while they talked together, horses and a chariot made of fire suddenly appeared between them and divided them. Then came the sound of a whirlwind, and, in the fire and the whirlwind, Elijah was carried up to heaven and was no longer seen by his disciple. Only his long cloak had fallen from his shoulders, and it lay upon the ground. Elisha lifted it wonderingly and reverently, as something left to him by his great teacher.

From that time, the power of Elijah entered Elisha, and he was able to work the same kind of miracles. There were other prophets in Israel, but none so powerful. All the good people who loved God looked to Elisha to help them. So he was not at all surprised when one day a poor woman, the widow of a dead prophet, came to him in great distress to ask for aid.

"Thy servant, my husband, is dead," she said pitifully, "Thou knowest that he was a good man. But he was poor, and he died owing money, and the man to whom he owed the money has come to take my two little sons, and he will sell them, my children whom I love, to be slaves!"

For this was done in those days, if anyone owed money when he died, and if his sons were too young to work and pay off the debt. So the poor widow was in the deepest distress. Elisha looked at her compassionately, and answered:

"Let me think what I can do for you. What have you in your house?"

The woman shook her head sadly. "I have nothing!" she said. "Just one little pot of oil!"

Then Elisha gave her a very strange command. "Go and borrow all the pots, and the jugs, and the basins, and the drinking cups that you can," said he. "Visit all your friends, and ask them to lend you every empty dish they have. Then go back into your house and shut the door, with no one but yourself and your sons inside. Set to work to fill the things you have borrowed by pouring out from your little pot of oil! And put them aside, as you fill them, one by one."

So the poor widow did as Elisha told her. She nearly filled the one room of her little house with all the jugs and vases and big bowls that she borrowed from her friends. Then she and her sons shut the door and drew the curtains, and the little boys brought the rest of the borrowed dishes to their mother to be filled.

The widow lifted the small pot and began to pour the oil into the big bowl that the children held. She poured and poured until it was full! Then the little boys put it carefully on one side and brought another. She filled that also, and so it went on, as her sons, wide-eyed with astonishment, brought basin after basin to her side, and she said, "Bring me yet more!" Then one of the children answered:

"There is not another basin!"

Then she looked into the little pot and saw that, at last, it was empty!

So the poor widow opened the door of the house, and went out and told the man of God. He said: "Go, sell the oil, pay the debt, and with the rest of the money live with thy children in peace!"

A little time later, Elisha came to a place called Shunem, where a rich woman lived. Whenever he passed her house, she would ask him in to eat and drink. At last she had a little chamber built for the prophet against the wall of the house. She put a bed in it, with a chair and a table and a candlestick, so that he could stop there at any time to rest and sleep. For she knew that he was a man of God, and that he moved through the land working miracles in one place or another, and she wished to show her respect for him in every way she could.

In return for her kindness, Elisha promised that she should have a little son – the child for whom she had longed for many, many years. How glad and happy she was, and how she loved and cherished her little boy when he was born! All the time the small room was kept furnished and cared for, against the wall of the house, so that Elisha could get to it whenever he liked.

One day, when the son of the sweet Shunammite

lady had grown into a fine little lad, his father took him down into one of his fields to watch the reapers. It was terribly hot, and the hot sun beat down upon the child's curls. All at once, he fell down, crying out:

"My head! oh, my head!"

The father, in deep distress, had the little boy carried home to his mother. She took him into her arms and sat there, silently nursing him, until noon; and at noon he died.

Then without a word or a tear, but with her face full of calm trust, she herself carried him to Elisha's little room against the wall. She laid him down on the prophet's narrow bed and went out, shutting the door behind her.

Calling to her husband, she said: "Tell one of the servants to saddle a donkey and to come with me. I am going to the man of God!"

When her husband asked why, she only answered: "It shall be well."

So, followed by the servant, she rode away, twenty miles across the hot plain to Mount Carmel, where she knew Elisha was to be found.

Elisha saw her coming and sent his servant, Gehazi, to meet her, and to ask if all was well with her husband and child. But she only answered, hurriedly, "It is well," and rode on.

Then, when she finally reached Elisha, she dismounted, and fell at his feet, and told him what had happened.

Elisha gave Gehazi his staff, and sent him on to the house of the Shunammite lady, and told him to lay the staff on the face of the child. So Gehazi went. But the child's mother would not go with him.

"As the Lord liveth, I will not leave thee!" she told Elisha. At last Elisha rose up and followed her.

As they drew near to the house, Gehazi met them. He told them that he had laid the staff on the face of the child, but that he had not awakened.

Then Elisha himself went alone into his own room, where the little boy lay, and shut the door. He prayed, and stretched himself tenderly over the child, mouth to mouth, eyes to eyes, and hands to hands, and the cold little boy began to grow warm.

Elisha stood up again then, and walked about, and prayed. Then, once more, he pressed the little child closely to him. And the boy sneezed seven times, and opened his eyes!

Then Elisha called Gehazi, and said to him: "Fetch his mother!"

And when she came, he told her: "Take up thy son!"

Then the good and gracious lady of the Shunammites went in and bowed down, and knelt at the feet of Elisha; and, when she had bent before him in deep silence for a few minutes, she took her living, loving little son in her arms and went out.

"GOD SAVE THE KING!"

ing Ahab and Jezebel had a daughter who was named the Princess Athaliah. When she grew up, she married the King of Judah. Very likely, she brought great riches with her, for we know that the royal family to which Jezebel belonged owned many palaces, full of exquisitely carved wood, and seats of mother-of-pearl, and ivory couches inlaid with precious stones.

When the new Queen Athaliah went to Jerusalem as a bride, she lived in a beautiful queen's house which had been built by Solomon for an Egyptian princess who was one of his wives. And, strangely enough, this house was made of cedar trees which the servants of Athaliah's own people, the people of Sidon, had cut down for Solomon in the woods of Mount Lebanon, far away in the north.

So Athaliah lived in her cedar palace and looked out of the windows at the peacocks and fountains in the Queen's garden. There were hundreds of horses to pull her chariots, and big camels who munched straw and barley in the stables. Her son Ahaziah grew up there, and he ruled over Judah after his father, Athaliah's husband, was dead; and this Queen, whose people, as you know, had prayed to the sun and the moon, tried to teach the young King Ahaziah to do the same. But a great captain of the army, Jehu, killed Ahaziah, and then the Queen-mother began to rule at Jerusalem herself. Ahaziah had been her only son, and she was afraid that the people would crown one of the other young princes as their King, and that then she herself would be left without any power at all. So she had all the royal children secretly put to death, set herself upon the throne of David, placed his crown upon her head, and took his royal mace in her hand.

But there was, at the Temple, a High Priest named Jehoiada, whose wife was of the family of the Kings. She took one tiny royal baby, only a year old, and hid him, with his nurse, in a room in one of the priests' houses that clustered all around the holy building, and there the little baby stayed, concealed from everybody, for six years.

He must have been rather like another tiny Samuel, as he trotted through the cedar-roofed rooms after the kind High Priest who brought him up. Jehoiada watched him, and loved him, and taught him very carefully. For the High Priest intended that this little child should be crowned King of Judah, as was his lawful right.

The little boy's name was Joash, or Jehoash, and, on his seventh birthday, the great day came. The High Priest brought him from his nursery and took him along dim and wonderful corridors lit with sparkling lamps. Then the little child found himself among carved pillars, and high golden screens, and purple hangings, with a sweet smell of spices lingering in the air. A group of grave men, all in battledress, stood nearby and gazed down upon him earnestly, as the High Priest, holding Joash by the hand, told them that here was the only living son of Jerusalem's lawful Kings.

They all took a vow of loyalty to the wondering child and went away. Then Joash trotted back to his nurse, and you may be sure he told her all about it. The following Sabbath morning, a great, though quiet, movement of troops came up to the King's house, and the Queen's house, and the House of God. The people who were getting ready to go and worship only saw what was quite usual – the doorkeepers of the Temple massing together to exchange their watch. But these men were all soldiers of the captains who had taken the oath of loyalty, and they were gathering in companies to defend the tiny King.

Inside the Temple, a wonderful thing was happening.

Once more, the kind, strong High Priest went to where little Joash waited in the chamber with his nurse. The child was fresh and sweet and fair in fine linen garments, with a little royal robe upon his shoulders. Again Jehoiada led him through the lamp-lit corridors into the Temple, where a number of people had gathered for worship, not knowing what was going to happen on this wonderful Sabbath.

Little Joash would see beautiful things, among them the heads and horns of twelve oxen made of shining brass and facing north, south, east and west. They held on their great glittering shoulders a gigantic bowl in which were carved the waves of a golden sea. This mighty bowl was shaped like a cup, and lilies were carved upon the rim. From one end of the Temple to the other, faithful captains stood shoulder to shoulder in a silent, watchful row. Every captain had a shield and a spear which had once belonged to King David upon his breast and in his right hand, and down this long row of rigid warriors, the High Priest led the startled child.

On the other side of the Temple court was a

The people shouted, "God save the king!" (page 147)

From the depths of the den came Daniel's voice (page 159)

hushed and waiting crowd of people, surprised into deep silence by what they saw.

Jehoiada took King David's crown and set it upon little Joash's head, and, for a moment, laid the big heavy parchment rolls, which held the list of the people, in his chubby arms. Then the High Priest poured the sacred, sweet-smelling oil upon the boy's soft hair and turned him to face the people. The men who were standing ready with their trumpets blew a great blast, the people clapped their hands, and right up to the roof of the Temple rang the mighty shout:

"God save the King!"

Queen Athaliah, from her garden of peacocks, heard the shouts and the trumpetings inside the Temple, and called her bodyguards and her maids-in-waiting, and went to the House of the Lord. The people made way for the Queen's procession, which passed through them to where the armed captains watched in their silent ranks in front of the shining oxen of brass. Queen Athaliah looked, and behold, in the royal place by the King's pillar stood a small, grave, wondering child, crowned with a crown of gold. Even as she caught sight of him, the trumpets sounded once more, and again the people shouted:

"God save the King!"

Queen Athaliah turned around angrily to the

crowd behind. "Treason!" she cried in a shrill, high voice. "Treason!" She thought that her subjects might yet rally to her; but no one stirred. She made a fierce signal to her bodyguards, but they looked at the captains by the altar, with the swords and spears of David, and they drooped their heads. Then the High Priest raised his hands commandingly.

"Take her!" he said to the captains. "Take her away from this holy place, and let her be put to her death!"

So the captains closed around Athaliah and marched out of the Temple with the wicked Queen in their midst. They led her down the long hill up which the horses were driven to the King's stables, and out of the shadows of the Temple into the sunshine on the slope below. There they put her to death, for had she not killed the royal princes six years ago? And Joash, the little King, very child of the Temple, grew up wise and good under the tender teaching of Jehoiada, the High Priest of God.

THE CAPTIVE MAID

he Bible tells how foreign armies came into the Kingdom of Israel; among them the armies of the King of Syria, whose country was not far from the mountains of Lebanon, where the spreading cedar trees grew. He was always sending bands of soldiers into Samaria; they stole the people's sheep and oxen, and sometimes the young boys and girls for slaves. Among the children who were taken away was a little maid.

This little maid had fallen into the hands of a captain called Naaman, who was strong and valiant, and much loved by his royal master, the Syrian King. Naaman gave the child to his wife, a rich and kind lady; to be her small servant and to wait upon her in her beautiful house at Damascus. The little girl was quite happy and soon learned to love her new master and mistress; for, although they had taken her far from her own people, they treated her very well. And often, as she helped her mistress to dress, or brought her fruit and wine to eat and drink, she would chatter about the land of Samaria, where the Holy Tent had once stood on Shiloh, and where the ivory palace built by Ahab still gleamed among the oaks of the high hills.

Now, although Naaman was a strong man, and a brave captain of soldiers, he had a terrible disease called leprosy, which made his skin white and dry and painful. The little maid used to look at him sorrowfully whenever he came her way, for she knew that his wife felt dreadfully unhappy about this sad disease. And one day, when she was with her mistress, the child said how much she wished that Naaman were in Samaria, where there was a great prophet who would cure him of his sickness.

The rich Syrian lady began quickly to ask the child questions, which she answered as well as she could. So Naaman got to hear that there was a prophet in Israel who could heal every kind of disease. Then the King of Syria himself was told of this wonderful man. The King took it for granted that the wonder of miracles could be no other than a King.

So he wrote a letter to the King of Israel, asking him to make Naaman healthy and strong again. He gave this letter to the Syrian captain and told him to take it to Samaria himself.

Naaman said goodbye to his wife, and set out in a

beautiful chariot drawn by five strong horses, taking a lot of silver and gold, and fine silk clothing, as presents to the monarch who had it in his power to make sick people well again.

The little maid watched him go. But she herself knew nothing of the King in his palace, with his courtiers and musicians about him. She only knew of the Holy Man, who wandered in his sandals over the mountains or slept in a little cave on the side of a hill.

Naaman, grand in his chariot, went driving up to the palace gates when he had reached his journey's end, and he gave the letter, rather haughtily, to the King of Israel. The King, when he had read it, was in despair. "For," he said, "who am I to cure a man of leprosy? Only God can do such things! The King of Syria is seeking a quarrel with me, that, once more, he may make war upon my country and myself."

Who could tell what would have happened after this, if Elisha had not heard that a great captain had come, in a chariot with horses, all the way from Syria, to be cured of leprosy? Happily, the prophet was told of the proud and determined visitor; and he sent a quiet message, bidding Naaman leave the palace and come into the open mountains. So, by and by, the big Syrian chariot thundered up to the door of the small dwelling place where, at the moment, the prophet lived. How glad the little maid would have been if she could have seen the chariot there, for she must have often thought of her kind foreign master looking for the holy man of God among the vineyards and pomegranate orchards of her own home.

Outside the house, Naaman waited. He expected Elisha would come out to him, stretch forth a powerful wand like a magician's, make loud cries to God, and so perform a wonderful and miraculous cure for everybody to see. But the prophet did not even stir from the chamber where he sat. He just sent out a message:

"Go and wash seven times in the River Jordan, and thy flesh shall come back to thee, and thou shalt be well!"

Then Naaman was very angry and went right away from the little home in the hills. If he had been told to wash in one of the great rivers of his own country, he would not have been so offended. But what was the River Jordan – what were all the waters of Israel to a captain of the mighty Syrian King? Naaman was inclined to go straight home again, but his servants persuaded him against this hurried return.

"If the prophet had told our master to do a great thing, he would have done it!" they said. "Why not, then, do a thing as small and easy as this?"

So Naaman was persuaded out of his anger, and he went down to the Jordan instead of hurrying home. His servants helped him to take off his fine clothes and stood on the bank, while, seven times, he dipped beneath the warm and limpid waters of the river of Israel. When he came up from the stream, treading the flowers of the bank underfoot, his flesh was as fair and soft and beautiful as the flesh of the little maid herself, through whose innocent chatter and loving memory of her own good Israelite prophet, the mighty captain of Syrian soldiers had been made whole.

DANIEL
AND THE LIONS

n the days of long ago, there was a magnificent city called Babylon, through the middle of which flowed the River Euphrates. The city had great walls around it, and many fine houses and a hundred shining brass gates inside its walls. The King's palace was especially fine, and the different monarchs who lived there were very proud of the wonders of their city, and often spoke of it as Babylon the Great.

But among the treasures of Babylon were many things that had been stolen from the Temple at Jerusalem – pillars of brass, ornaments of silver, and an exquisite screen carved to look like pomegranate fruit and flowers. The armies of Babylon had conquered the city of David and made prisoners of many of her people.

One of these prisoners was a beautiful boy called Daniel, who was as fair to look at as David had been, and full of the quiet wisdom of God.

This boy from Jerusalem was a little Prince in his

own country, for he was a member of the family of the Jewish Kings. The courtiers and governors of the great palace at Babylon brought him up very carefully, for they wanted to make him one of themselves. But Daniel never forgot his own people, and the God about whom he had learned in the lovely Temple that held the Ark of the Promise. As he grew older, his wisdom and his goodness increased, so that he was able to do things that other people could not do; and, like Joseph of old, he could tell the meaning of dreams.

Well, as time went on, the King of Babylon inquired what had become of the beautiful boy from Jerusalem and his other little royal companions. So the courtiers brought them to him as he sat on his throne. The boys had grown up into young men now, and the King found them, in wisdom and understanding, ten times better than all the learned old magicians and teachers that he kept around him at his court. So he always had the young men near him; and Daniel, who was wiser than any of the others, became at last the head of the company of advisers. He was named "Master of the Magicians," and he wore a beautiful scarlet robe, and a glittering gold chain hung around his neck and fell almost to the hem of the crimson gown.

He stayed at the court in great pomp and state during the reign of two Kings. He explained to them the mysterious power of Jehovah, and told them what was right and what was wrong. So the Kings said of him that the spirit of the gods was in him, and that no secret was hidden from his eyes.

Then a King came to the throne of Babylon who was named Darius; and Daniel stayed with Darius, and helped and strengthened him. Darius was ruler over many people beyond Babylon; among these people were the Medes and Persians. They all looked to Darius – who was a Mede himself by birth – to act wisely and justly in the land. So he set a hundred and twenty princes over the whole kingdom, and three presidents over the princes; and Daniel was the chief president of all.

But, as so often happens, the hundred and twenty princes and the two other presidents grew jealous of Daniel and plotted to destroy him. They said:

"He does no wrong! He is faithful and true, and the people love him! We can only do him harm through the law of his God!"

So they went to Darius, and praised his kingly greatness, and his power of making everybody happy, and said they had thought of a way by which he could make himself still more popular.

"O King Darius!" they said, "let no one, for thirty days, ask tokens of anyone but thee! Let no one petition either God or man for help except thy great and glorious self! Make a decree that this be so and that whoever disobeys shall be thrown into the den of lions! Write it in thine own handwriting and seal it with thine own seal!"

So King Darius, quite unsuspecting, and believing that the hundred and twenty princes and the two presidents were advising him in all purity of heart, wrote the decree and sealed it with his seal; and it became a law of the Medes and Persians.

Daniel, like everybody else, heard about the new order given by King Darius. He just smiled quietly to himself and went to the open windows of his house, and prayed there three times a day, as usual, with his face turned towards Jerusalem. All the people in the street below saw the master of the magicians, the greatest ruler in the land after Darius himself, quietly kneeling in his window in his scarlet robe and golden chain, and making petitions to God in defiance of the unalterable command of the King.

Then, in great triumph, the princes and presidents hurried to Darius and told him that Daniel – the beloved and trusted Daniel – had himself broken a law of the Medes and Persians! Darius saw that he had been tricked, and his heart was nearly broken. Until the sun went down, he tried to persuade his counsellors to let him withdraw the decree, but they would not.

So then, at sunset, the King sent for Daniel and told him that he must be cast into the den of lions. Daniel answered nothing, and the sad procession, headed by the King, went from the throne room down the steps to the great strong den where the royal lions were kept. And Daniel was thrown into the midst of them.

Then, even as the men flung him to the savage tawny beasts, they watched from their corners with wide mysterious eyes, the King's voice broke out in a great cry of faith and hope, as he called to the magician whom he loved:

"Thy god, whom thou servest continually, *He* will deliver thee!" cried the sad King. Then a great stone was brought and rolled in front of the door of the den, and the King sealed it with his own signet ring and went miserably away.

All night long, Darius could not sleep. He had neither food nor drink, and ordered his musicians to keep away from him. He thought of nothing but Daniel, and very early in the morning, he left his fine bedchamber and hurried down the steps again to the terrible den. There he cried out in anguish:

"O Daniel, servant of the living god, is thy God, whom thou servest continually, able to deliver thee from the lions?"

And then, out of the depths of the den, came Daniel's own voice:

"O King, live forever! My God hath sent His angel, and hath shut the lions' mouths, that they might not hurt me!"

Then the King, with great joy, sent for his servants and the keepers, and they opened the den, and Daniel came out. Darius ordered those who had accused Daniel to be thrown to the lions in his place, and the mighty monarch proclaimed throughout his whole kingdom the power of the God of Daniel, who could work great marvels, and who had delivered His faithful servant from the lions.

THE
NEW
TESTAMENT

GLAD TIDINGS OF GREAT JOY

Many centuries had passed since Daniel prayed in his window at Babylon, looking towards Jerusalem, the holy city, where the Temple of Jehovah stood. Strange, sad happenings had brought much sorrow to the Israelites in the Promised Land. Only a few of the chosen people lingered among the olive-covered hills and on the grassy slopes where Abraham, Isaac, and Jacob had watched their flocks clustering around the wells. Foreign kings had ruled over these poor, deserted fragments of Abraham's great nation. Many strangers had come to live in the midst of them. But always the sons of Israel dreamed of a great King, their Saviour, who would rise up to bring them together again under his protection and bring back the glories of David to the Promised Land.

And, one starry night, the Saviour came.

The sun had set on the plains near Bethlehem, the little old town where David had lived and Ruth had gleaned in the barley fields so long ago. The wide, dark fields were covered with sleeping flocks of sheep. Small folds, like huts, were built all around, and some of the pretty fluffy creatures had crept inside with their lambs. Others were resting outside in the quiet open air. Their shepherds sat by the folds, watching the shadowy flocks and listening to the tinkling sound of a little brook that ran through the hills nearby.

As they sat there, a sudden brilliant light, strange and lovely, seemed to fall around them from nowhere and to send their shadows, long and dark, upon the rough grass. As they looked around, startled and wondering, they saw that the light came from a beautiful angel, who stood in the midst of it. The shepherds were very frightened. But the angel spoke to them in a voice that was joyful and kind.

"Fear not!" he said. "Behold, I bring you good tidings of great joy, which shall be to all people. For unto you is born this day in the city of David, a Saviour, which is Christ the Lord. And this shall be a sign unto you, ye shall find the Babe wrapped in swaddling clothes, lying in a manger!"

He finished speaking, and all at once the whole sky and earth seemed to be filled with many more angels. Their wings were like golden light, and their robes seemed to be made of stars.

"Behold, I bring you glad tidings of great joy" (page 162)

The Wise Men adored Him and gave Him gifts (page 171)

And they praised God, saying;

"Glory to God in the Highest, and on Earth peace, goodwill towards men!"

The shepherds looked, and listened, and held their breath, as the great song swept out over the plains and hills. Then, gradually, the beautiful music died away, the shining vision faded, and nothing could be heard but the little stream, nothing seen but the dark slumbering forms of the sheep.

Then the shepherds turned to each other in wonder.

"We will go to Bethlehem," they said. "Bethlehem is the city of David. There, too, are the stables of the inn, where mangers are built for the oxen and the donkeys to eat from. The angels sang of a wonderful new born Babe whom we should find in a manger. We will go and see."

So they took their staffs and set off up the rocky paths towards the white houses of Bethlehem glimmering under the sky. There they went at once to the inn. It was in a little square, around an open space where the cattle belonging to guests could lie down and sleep. The guests themselves found shelter in small rough rooms, set right against the outside walls and kept dry with a thatched roof. The shepherds, as soon as they reached this strange inn, began to ask if any wonderful child was to be found there.

Nobody knew of one. But some people said that two people from the country, a man named Joseph, and his wife Mary, had arrived at the inn too late to find an empty room, and so had taken shelter in one of the caves just outside which was used as a stable. And they said that Mary had had a baby born there, and that the shepherds could find them if they went to look.

So the shepherds went away again into the darkness, past the closed doors of the guests' huts, past the donkeys and oxen lying asleep in the big square yard. When they got outside, they gazed around the slope of the hill to see if they could see the cave. A few paces off, among the dim shapes of the white high rocks, they saw a feeble light. So they felt their way along the road in its direction and found themselves at the opening of the cave.

The light came from a small clay lamp, shaped like a saucer, with a burning wick floating on the oil. It shone softly on the rocky limestone roof of the cave and on the dim figures of a man and a woman inside. More softly still, it shone on the face of a tiny baby, who lay wrapped in swaddling clothes in the manger, fast asleep.

The shepherds knew that they had found what they had come to seek, and that the baby was the Saviour, who was Christ the Lord. They looked at the tiny sleeping face in great, glad awe. Then they answered the questions of Joseph and Mary, who stared in amazement at the strange men gathered, whispering, at the open entrance of the little rocky cave.

They explained to Joseph and Mary what had happened on the plains just below Bethlehem. They told the story of the bright angels, and the thrilling song that had swept through the night and died away at last in the stars. When they had explained it all, they turned to other people who had come out from the inn and stopped near the cave, and told the story all over again. Then they went back to their sheep, praising God for the things that they had seen and heard that night.

Mary, the mother of the Lord Jesus, kept all these things down in her heart, and thought of them nearly always as she watched her little sleeping child.

THREE WISE MEN FROM THE EAST

ow, in Jerusalem, Solomon's palace had long ago been destroyed, but there was a big and beautiful building in its place, high above the hilly streets. Its rooms were magnificently decorated, and court after court led into each other; some had cedar roofs, others were open, like walled gardens, to the sky. There were cypress trees, dark and tall, and all kinds of fruit and flowers, and rose-fringed fountains with beautiful bronze figures, and doves which looked like opals flying around the shining pools. Herod, the King, who had built the new palace, lived there, surrounded by servants dressed in rich silken robes.

What a different place from the little cave with the tiny manger at Bethlehem!

Herod, although he followed the Jewish religion, was not a Jew by birth. He was allowed to call himself the Jewish King by the Romans, who were masters now in Palestine, but the Jews themselves did not consider him their king. Herod had heard it said that some day the Jews would again have a King from their own people. He thought this meant that he would not be able to reign in his magnificent palace any more.

Well, a few weeks after the shepherds had seen the angels, Herod heard something that made all his former worries more real and perplexing. His servants told him that there were, in Jerusalem, certain Wise Men who had journeyed there from their own countries in the East, where they were almost like kings. They were asking where the new King of the Jews had been born, because, they said, they had seen in the East a strange and glorious star, and, knowing that this meant the birth of a very great King, they had come all the way from where they lived to worship Him.

Everyone in Jerusalem was talking about the Wise Men, though the people in the city had not yet heard of the angels that the shepherds had seen at Bethlehem. So Herod sent for the Chief Priests, and the Scribes, and asked them to come to the palace and talk the matter over with him.

The Chief Priests were Jews who helped Herod govern; the Scribes were people like lawyers. *They* too, knew, that prophets had said, long ago, that a wonderful new King should reign over the Children of Israel. So when Herod, sitting on his throne, asked them where this great King, who was called Christ, should be born, they were able to say that it was to be in Bethlehem.

Herod let them go without asking anything more. But he found out where the Wise Men were staying, sent for them secretly, and talked to them about the star and its meaning. Then he, himself, told them to go to Bethlehem.

"Go," he said, "and search diligently for the young child, and when ye have found him, bring me word again, that I may come and worship him, also."

But Herod's heart was very wicked as he spoke, because he meant to kill the baby Christ if he could find him. However, the Wise Men did not know this, so they set out, as he had told them, for Bethlehem.

No sooner had they started their journey, riding on camels with their servants behind them, than lo! they saw again in the sky the great shining star that they had seen in the East! It went ahead of them, trembling in a diamond glitter, until it stopped above a little house among the hills. Then it stood quite still and hung, sparkling with light, in the deep blue of the night sky; this little house was the place where the Baby Jesus now lived.

Mary and Joseph, of course, had been visitors in

Bethlehem. They had gone there the night the baby Jesus was born, so that Joseph might be "taxed," or have his name written down in a kind of census, according to a new law that had been passed. A lot of other people – shepherds, and cheesemakers, and men who worked in vineyards – had gone there for the same reason. It was because of this great crowd of people that Joseph and Mary had not been able to find room at the inn. But now the census had been taken, and they were living in a little house among the hills, with nothing to mark it from other places except the great dazzling star.

When the Wise Men reached the starlit house, they got down from their camels and asked if they might go in. When they saw Mary, the fair young mother, with the little baby in her arms, they fell down and adored Him.

Then they called their servants, and there, in the little peasant's cottage, they opened their parcels of treasures. They gave gifts to the tiny infant King – gold, beautiful and precious, and sweet-smelling delicate spicy fragrances in little bowls, called frankincense and myrrh. They worshipped Him all the time, kneeling on the baked clay floor. Then they rose and went out once more into the night, and the bright star from the East still hung shining in the sky.

THE FLIGHT
INTO EGYPT

he Wise Men left the little house where Joseph and Mary lived with the baby Jesus and went back on their camels to Jerusalem. As they rode slowly through the night, along the rough roads pale with dust and often strewn with stones, they must have looked back, sometimes, to where the beautiful star hung over the Lord Jesus's quiet village home.

The gates and roofs of Jerusalem were some way off, so the Wise Men made a camp in the hills for the rest of the night. You see, they had come from countries on the other side of many plains and valleys; and they carried their tents, their food, and their servants and kitchens, with them.

The servants set up the big, comfortable tents, and the Wise Men went to rest. Then two angels of God came back to the hills and plains near Bethlehem.

They did not come, this time, in rainbows of light, with a great sweet anthem of gladness. They trod softly, and with folded wings, through the darkness.

One of them passed the servants who guarded the entrance of the tent where the Wise Men slept, lifted the fine inner curtains, and crossed the grassy floor on which rich mats were laid. Then he stooped and whispered a dream into the ears of the sleeping Kings.

The dream the angel whispered told them that they must not go back to Jerusalem – must not tell Herod where the royal baby was to be found. They listened in their sleep, and, when they woke in the morning, they knew that an angel had whispered.

So they obeyed the dream from God, and, rising, told their servants to fold the tents, pack up the food, and prepare for a long journey. Looking back towards the house of Joseph and Mary, they saw that the bright star had faded in the dawn. The Wise Men never went back to Jerusalem, but returned to their own countries by another way.

The other angel that came that night went to the little home under the great star.

He, too, crept softly, with folded wings, inside the door. Mary and Jospeh and the baby Jesus were all fast asleep, with one little candle burning in the room. But presently Joseph stirred in his slumber, and half-opened his tired eyes.

He must have thought at first that the oil lamp was

burning with a strange beauty, for the room was full of misty golden light. He opened his eyes more fully and saw in his dream the glistening of white robes. Then it seemed as if the soft wings of some great bird fanned his face. Sitting up on his low mattress, he saw that an angel of God was in the room.

The angel had a grave, beautiful face, and spoke earnestly. "Joseph," he said, "arise! Take the young child and his mother, and flee into Egypt, and be thou there until I bring thee word. For Herod will seek the young child to destroy Him."

When the angel had spoken, his earnest face, his white robes, and his shining wings began to grow dim. He faded from Joseph's sight, and only the light of the little lamp was in the room.

Joseph knew that he must obey the vision of the angel. The Baby had already been taken to the Temple at Jerusalem to be blessed and had been named Jesus. Joseph remembered all this and knew how angry Herod must be to think that another King had been born in the land. So he woke Mary, and, in the cold dawn, they began to put their things together. All day, they made their preparations, and, when night came, Joseph brought a donkey to the door of the little house. Mary came out with the baby Jesus, Joseph helped her to mount, and he led the donkey away through the night, down the hilly path, to the long, long road that led to Egypt.

Then they were gone, and the Wise Men were gone also. Herod found that nobody could tell him where the little King of the Jews was. He was so angry that he had all the babies under two years old in Bethlehem killed immediately. But the Infant Christ was safe in Egypt.

Joseph and Mary stayed in Egypt safely until Herod died. Then, one night, the angel appeared again in their little chamber and told Joseph that he could now take the baby back. But when Joseph found out that Herod's son was reigning in his father's place, he felt that it would not be safe to go back to Bethlehem. While he was wondering what to do, the angel came to him a third time.

This third time, the angel told him to go and live for good in the north of the Holy Land, in a place called Nazareth. So Joseph and Mary turned aside from Bethlehem on their return journey and went and settled in Nazareth, a strange high town built on the side of a mountain which had once been a volcano.

It was here that Joseph set up again in business as a carpenter, and the little baby, who was to become so great and wonderful, grew to be a boy.

ANGELS OF GLORY IN THE TEMPLE

mong the many stories about Mount Moriah, where Herod's Temple now stood in the sunlight, are three stories of angels. The first was the guardian of little Isaac, whose voice saved the child and blessed his trusting father, Abraham. The second angel appeared to David. The third was Gabriel himself, the great angel of whom Daniel used to dream, whose wings were wide, whose flight was swift and sure, and whose face was turned always towards the glory of God.

You can read about the second angel in the stories of David, the King and sweet psalmist of Israel. This messenger from God stood on the heights of the mountain at a time when there was much sickness in the land of Canaan. A drawn sword was in his hand, stretched out over Jerusalem. The place on which his feet rested was a threshing floor, flat, rocky, and open to the winds. And David, the King, saw this Angel of Death and fell on his face and prayed. Then the great angel sheathed his sword, spread his wings, and floated away; and the sickness was stopped. David bought the threshing floor and had an altar built there to the Lord, and around this altar, Solomon built the wonderful temple you know about. The Ark of God's Promise was brought there and set up in the Holy Place, behind the curtain called the Veil.

But Solomon's beautiful Temple was broken down and burned by a mighty King who brought big armies to fight against Israel from the land of the Chaldees, and the Ark of Jehovah was probably buried in the burning ruin. As the Lord had first spoken in the holy fires of a mountain, so in the unholy fires of another mountain His glory seemed to pass away. His people were carried as captives to Babylon, and many of them stayed there under the rule of the great Persian kings.

Then one of these Persian kings, who was named Cyrus, gave an order that the Temple of Jehovah, the God of Israel, was to be rebuilt. A man named Zerubbabel set up the altar again and built God's house around it, with three rows of great stones and with timber from the King's own forests. Many of the gold and silver ornaments were brought back from Babylon but the Ark of the Covenant, with the holy Tablets of the Law inside it, was never again seen in the Temple of Jerusalem.

Zerubbabel's Temple – or, as some call it, the Temple of Nehemiah, who wrote a great book about it – lasted for five hundred years.

Then, some time before the baby Christ was born, Herod promised the people that he would set up a Temple even greater than that of Solomon – a building of snowy marble and glittering brass. To the altar in the heart of this still unfinished Temple, where carpenters and carvers were busy pulling down the quiet old courts of Zerabbabel and setting up the splendid new walls of Herod, the angel Gabriel came.

The angel showed himself at the hour of the evening service. A priest called Zacharias stood alone in the Holy Place. From the outer courts came the long, low murmur of hundreds of people at prayer. Zacharias was holding high the vessel of incense, from which the pale smoke wreathed about the altar, and the perfume of crushed spices rose. Suddenly, to the right of the altar, shone Gabriel's wings of light. It must have seemed to Zacharias, for a moment, as if Jehovah had descended once more upon the Mercy Seat, as in the days of old.

Gabriel told Zacharias that a son would shortly be born to him, who would be the prophet of the Highest, who would prepare the way for the coming

Messiah, the God-given King of the Jews. In due
time this son of Zacharias was born. He was John the
Baptist, and he did prepare the hearts of the people
for Jesus Christ.

Well, you may be sure that the story of the angel
Gabriel got told and retold, and many priests who
served in the Temple, and many faithful men and
women who came there daily to pray, were waiting
eagerly for the birth of the promised King.

One of these old people was called Simeon.
Everybody knew he was a good and upright man;
and on a certain day, just four weeks after the birth of
the Holy Child at Bethlehem, Simeon felt something
within urging him to go to the Temple. He was so old
that the way seemed long to his tired feet, but,
leaning on his staff, he mounted the steep steps and
reached a court with high columns all around it,
which he entered through two great brass doors,
called the Beautiful Gate. This court was the Court
of the Women, and many women and children, and
priests, and singers, were passing to and fro, shoeless,
over the marble floor. Simeon waited, and by and by
his eyes fell upon a little group coming towards him –
a man, a fair, gentle woman, and a tiny baby held
tenderly in the woman's arms.

The young mother paused and dropped some

coins into a large box shaped like a trumpet which stood against the wall. The money was a thanks offering for her first-born Son, and was just as much as she would have paid for two pigeons, which poor people, in those days, offered to God when He sent them their first little boy. Simeon watched her pause, and his eyes dwelt earnestly upon the Child that she carried. Then a vision unseen by the rest of the people in the Temple opened out for Simeon around the mother and the Child. The old man saw that the whole Temple was bathed in the Glory of God.

He went forward and took the tiny baby in his arms, and rapt words fell from his lips, while his face, so worn and furrowed, was radiant with joy.

"Lord, now lettest Thou Thy servant depart in peace, according to Thy word! For mine eyes have seen Thy salvation which Thou hast prepared before the face of all people! A light to lighten the Gentiles, and the glory of Thy people Israel!"

Joseph and Mary heard the words fall from Simeon's lips, and they looked, in grave wonder, from the old man to the little Child. Then Simeon placed the Holy Baby back in His mother's arms. He lifted high his hands and blessed the parents of the sacred infant that lay so calmly against Mary's breast. Simeon told them that the Child had been

Joseph took the Child and His mother to Egypt (page 175)

Jesus learned the carpenter's work from Joseph (page 184)

sent for a wonderful sign, and that, though many in Israel should fall away from Him, yet, through Him, they should rise again.

Then, just as Joseph and Mary were going to take the baby away, an old, old woman came slowly across the marble floor towards where the little group stood. She, too, saw the vision of beauty that seemed to surround them; and she echoed Simeon's poem of joy and gazed with glad eyes upon the child. And so, with the grave promises given by the aged pair ringing softly in their ears, Mary and Joseph left the Temple and went home.

After that, the Wise Men came and spread the news of the star, and the little baby Christ was, as you know, taken to Egypt, and then brought back to Nazareth, where he grew up in the grace of God.

"MY FATHER'S BUSINESS"

ary and Joseph were poor, and Joseph worked as a carpenter in Nazareth. He had all sorts of things to make – yokes and carts for the oxen, and the wooden parts of the strange Palestine implements.

As the Lord Jesus grew out of babyhood into boyhood, He began to learn the carpenter's work. He was taught to use hammers and axes and iron tools, just as Jospeh did. He must have thought, often, of how Joseph's ancestors worked for God. Among those ancestors was not only that very Bezaleel into whose heart Jehovah had put the wisdom and craftsmanship of a great artist, but also the architect Zerubbabel, who had set up the Temple that Herod was now pulling down to replace with his own magnificent building.

The Child, we read, was filled with wisdom. It dwelt in His heart, for He had come straight to the world from God Himself. There, working among the long, stripped logs of timber – trees brought perhaps from other countries in big ships, or cedars from Lebanon, or palms from Jericho – was the little boy who knew the secrets of the God who, in the Garden of Eden, had planted the Tree of Life. Perhaps as He cut and carved the wood He sang softly to Himself the song of Isaiah, with its fragrant promise: "I will plant in the wilderness the cedar, the shittah tree, and the myrtle and the oil tree! I will set in the desert the fir tree and the pine and the box tree together!"

We cannot tell what His thoughts were, but we know that as He grew in body, so He grew strong in spirit and was filled with the wisdom of God.

His mother must often have thought of Him, wonderingly, as she went about her daily work – grinding grain in the morning with the help of a friend, baking cakes from the flour, and going to the well at sunset to fill her pitchers with cool water. Each dawn, she would open the door of the little house wide, even before the sun had risen over the distant hills of Galilee. Each dusk she lit her lamp of oil and set it in the window. Then the family would gather for supper, and perhaps talk over the old tales of Israel.

Then came the day when the Holy Child was twelve years old – the age at which Jewish boys were taken for the first time to the great feasts held in the distant town of Jerusalem.

So the boy, Christ Jesus, set off with his parents on a three-day journey, through the hills and plains of Samaria, to the Temple on the Holy Hill, for the great festival of the Passover. The faithful Israelites who dwelt in Nazareth were not very many in number, but were enough to make up what were called "companies". These little groups kept together on the road, and shared food and lodgings. On the way up to Jerusalem, Jesus stayed with his parents. When they got there, everyone took offerings to the priests at the Temple. They said prayers there for three days, in memory of the time when Jehovah had brought them safely out of Egypt, and then they set off for home again.

There must have been a bit of crowding and pushing at the different gates of Jerusalem as all the companies, with their donkeys, and their carts, and their camels, set out soon after dawn to return to the homes that were scattered through the length and breadth of Palestine. In the confusion Mary and Joseph missed their young son. But they felt He must be among their friends from Nazareth, and they started without misgiving. As the day wore on, the road through Samaria grew quieter, emptied of all except those who were going in the direction of

Nazareth. Then Joseph began to move from group to group, seeking the boy Jesus. But He was nowhere to be found in the different companies. In dismay and anxiety, His parents turned back to Jerusalem.

For three days they sought Him in the busy city, searching through the sheep market, and the singers' houses, and the great theatre and hippodrome that the Greeks and Romans had built under Herod. But He was in none of these places. At last they found Him – where do you think? Within the holy shadows of the Temple of Jehovah itself!

He was seated, a young, slender, earnest boy, in the midst of the grave old doctors of learning. He was asking them all sorts of questions about the Books of the Law of Jehovah, and the story of the Holy Tent, and the rod of Aaron, and the Garden of Wonderful Trees. Sometimes He listened gravely to their answers. But sometimes He shook His young fair head. And all who listened to Him were amazed.

Then His parents drew near, rejoicing, though still hurt and grieved with the memory of their great anxiety. His mother told Him how long and how sorrowfully they had looked for Him. But His eyes were full of dreams as He heard her, and He tried to make her understand.

"I must be about My Father's business," He

explained earnestly; but Mary and Joseph did not know the meaning of it all.

Then, in obedience, after one last look around His Father's house, the boy Jesus went away with His parents, back to His earthly duty and His heavenly dreams, in the carpenter's shop on the slopes of the warm Nazarene hill.

The Bible does not tell us much about Christ until He was grown and began to go among the people, teaching them, loving them, healing their sick, and raising their dead. But we know just what Nazareth was like: that its slopes were green with vineyards, and its wild flowers as beautiful as those which grew all around the Sea of Galilee. The carpenter's shop was not part of Joseph's house, but would have been right in the middle of the bazaar, where, all day long, the people bought and sold. Those who wanted their tools mended, or made, or any planks sawn for their houses, would come to the shop and give their orders to Joseph; while the boy Jesus would stand listening, ready to help in any way that He could.

How little the people in the bazaar, talking, laughing, and bargaining, knew. They never even guessed that this earnest-faced child was the true Light of the World.

JOHN, THE YOUNG FISHERMAN

n the part of Palestine where the Lord Jesus grew up, there is a lake high up among the mountains – a lake so large that it is called the Sea of Galilee. Big hills slope down to its beaches, and the sand among the pebbles of the shore is made almost entirely of tiny crushed shells. These shells sparkle in the sunshine, and the little waves of the sea sparkle, too. The mountainsides are thick with flowers, and tall palm trees with plumy tops fringe the lanes.

One day, on the beach, a young fisherman sat mending his father's nets. Near him were his father, Zebedee, and his elder brother, James, and, a little way out from the shore, in a big boat, were two other fishermen named Simon Peter and Andrew, who were throwing a net into the sea.

It was very calm and still, and John, the young fisherman, was very busy. But suddenly the hush was broken. Footsteps came along the shingle, and a strong, clear, man's voice echoed out over the water:

"Simon Peter and Andrew, come! Follow me!"

Everybody on the beach looked up, John among them; and he saw that Christ was standing just at the edge of the waves.

Christ was grown now, and John thought he had never seen a man so strong and kind and beautiful. The fisherboy sat, his hands still holding the net, gazing earnestly, as Simon Peter and Andrew, without a word, pushed their boat nearer to the land, climbed out, and joined the Lord Jesus. Then Christ walked on and came to where the young fisher sat.

When He saw the lad, He loved him, perhaps because, as we know, John was so much younger than the other disciples. He held out one hand to the youth, and one to James, the elder brother. And He smiled and said, again: "Follow Me! You two also — follow Me!" James got up from the shingle, and John did likewise, and they joined the Lord Jesus and became His disciples.

They went with Him, nearly always, after that, to a great many villages, and to big cities, some on the coast where the large merchant-vessels lay in the ports, and some in the valleys where the grain grew all around. John liked the coast towns best, because of the ships that he saw there. But they always came back to the Sea of Galilee, where John's father and mother lived. The Lord Jesus lived there Himself, you see, at that time, at the small rocky town called Capernaum. Very often He fished with the fishermen, or went in their boats from one side of the great lake to the other.

They all knew that He was not like other men, just as He had not been quite like other children. They could tell, by the wonderful things He did, that God's power was in Him and around Him. John loved Him more and more every day of his life.

One day, Christ had been doing kind and wonderful things among the people on the shores of the lake. When evening came, He was tired, and He went up to the top of one of the hills to be by Himself and pray to His Father, under the blue sky. He told the fishermen not to wait for Him, but to spread their sails, and go home across the lake without Him. So they started off, just as the sun was setting, though, most likely, they knew that the moon would soon rise; and for a little while, they sailed calmly and softly towards Capernaum.

Then, as happens sometimes the wind suddenly changed. John heard the new sound in the breeze and looked up at the sails in dismay. Quickly all the fishermen pulled to the ropes and reefed the big sails, so that the storm should not upset the boat. They were only just in time. Down swept the wind, shrieking and whistling from the hilltops. It struck the water hard so that it began to lash itself into big white waves. These huge waves rolled against the side of the boat, and the fishermen had to take their oars and turn the bows of the boat into the wind to keep from being capsized. The moon rose over the hills, big and bright, except when it was hidden by the dark racing clouds which tore across the sky. John must have trembled as he helped to row the boat, for he would be very afraid.

One great cloud hid the face of the moon for several minutes, and nothing could be seen around the boat but dark shadowy caves of green water and white mists of foam. Then all at once the moon shone out again; and, walking on the tossing sea, down a path of silvery glory, the fishermen saw the figure of Jesus coming towards them from the land.

John caught his breath in silence. Then he heard exclamations from the other fishermen at their oars as they bent their back against the wind; and one cried out under his breath that he saw a Spirit. Another cried out, also under his breath, that it was the Lord Jesus. Simon Peter called out, louder than any of them, to that wonderful, beautiful figure in the moonlight on the sea:

"Lord, if it be Thou, bid me come unto Thee on the water!"

The answer rang out through the wind – "Come!"

And Simon Peter sprang out of the boat into the sea. Then his courage and his faith failed him, and, with a loud cry, he began to sink. John must have shut his eyes for a moment in fear.

Then, all at once, the wind fell. When John looked up again, he could see Jesus holding Simon Peter by His side, as both stood upon the waves. Together, in the sudden calm, the Master and His disciple stepped into the ship. But Jesus, as He supported Simon Peter, had rebuked him, very gently and softly, saying, "Oh, thou of little faith, wherefore didst thou doubt?"

THE LITTLE BOY'S FISHES AND LOAVES

Ou remember that, on the afternoon before Christ walked on the sea to join the fishermen in their boat, He had been doing many wonderful things, and had also been teaching the people about God, and about God's love for the world. He had been talking to them on the hills overlooking the Sea of Galilee, at the other end from where Capernaum stood. He had been making sick people well, and sorrowful people happy, and, while He was telling them how to be good and to obey God, more and more people came up the hillside paths to listen.

John, the fisher-boy, was there, of course, keeping as near to the Master as he could. And John watched the crowds climbing the mountainside from all parts of the surrounding countryside — men, and women, and children, toiling up in the hot sunshine. Then the fisher-boy saw ships crossing the lake, bringing more people. Even people walking on the road that ran through the high hills, stopped their camels and mules when they saw the crowd in the distance, and came up to see what was happening.

The Lord Jesus stood a little apart, among the rocks, where ferns and vines grew. His voice, as He spoke, rang out clearly, like a trumpet; for, in Palestine, you can hear every little sound from very far away. The people kept so quiet that, as well as that strong and beautiful voice, your ears might have caught the tinkle of the brooks and streams running down the hillside, and the rippling of the lake on the shore below.

At last, even the Master was tired, and He sat down, leaning back against the rocks with His eyes shut. But the people who had been listening did not go away. A few of them had brought something to eat – dates, and little cakes, and honey. On the edge of the crowd, some boys, who had come up from the villages on the plain, would be selling food out of baskets, just as you often see people selling things to eat at fairgrounds today.

But perhaps there were not many of these lads; their baskets would soon be emptied, and they would go away. At last, the Lord Jesus raised Himself from the rocks. He looked at the great crowd of people, and He turned to one of His disciples, who was named Philip, and asked:

"Where can we buy bread for all these tired, hungry people? They must want something to eat!"

Philip shook his head. The other disciples looked around, first at the people, and then at the green, soft hills.

"This is a place without houses or markets," they said. "Send the people away to the distant villages for food and shelter."

"No," the Lord Jesus said gently, "we cannot do that. We must find something for all of them to eat."

The disciples could not see any way of feeding the people, but at that moment a boy came walking along the mountain path. He had a basket in his hands, and he was carrying this basket very carefully, for it held five barley loaves and two small fishes. We are not told in the Bible what he meant to do with them. Perhaps he thought he could sell them – perhaps they were his own simple supper. By and by he saw the crowds of people on the slope of the hill, standing in rows, one above the other and looking like great groups of flowers, in their red and blue and green garments. He went straight up to Andrew, who was standing nearest, and thrust the precious basket into the fisherman's hands.

I think that, when the little boy saw the hungry people, and heard Christ's disciples say that there was no way in which they could be fed, he must have wanted to help, even though what he could give was so little. He must have been proud and happy, too, when Andrew took the basket. But the fisherman smiled and shook his head when he looked inside, and saw the little loaves and small broiled fishes. However, the loving eyes of the Master looked on the child with a promise in them.

"What has the child got?" asked the Lord Jesus.

They showed Him the basket and said that what was in it was no use among so many people. And the little boy stood by, perhaps feeling very sorry that he had not got more. But the Master held up His hand.

"Tell the people to sit down," He said; "and give the basket to Me!"

So the people sat on the grassy hillside, and the Lord Jesus stood up, took the basket, and, lifting His face towards the sky, He thanked God for the food and blessed it. Then He began to hand out the bread and fish from the basket. He went on, and on, and on; but the food did not come to an end. The disciples kept taking it to the people and coming back for more, and the little boy watched in amazement and joy. At last, everyone had had enough, and still the Lord held the basket in His hands.

"Now," He said, "gather up the pieces that the

people have let fall, so that nothing may be wasted."

When all the fragments had been picked up, there were twelve baskets full of broken food.

The the Lord Jesus probably turned with the sweetest smile, and gave the little boy his own small basket back again. And the child, as he went home in the sunset light, must have been filled with wonder at the things he had seen.

After three days, they found Him in the Temple (page 187)

A clear voice echoed over the water: "Come! Follow me!"
(page 190)

Christ was walking towards them on the tossing sea
(page 192)

The little boy handed his small basket to the disciple
(page 196)

THE STORY OF THE GOOD SAMARITAN

esus became well-known as a teacher, but there were always those who wanted to prove themselves cleverer that He was.

One day when Jesus was teaching a group of people, including many children, a lawyer came up to Him, hoping to trap Him with a clever question.

"What shall I do to gain eternal life?" he asked.

Jesus replied, "What do the scriptures tell you? How do you interpret them?"

The lawyer answered, "Love God with all your heart, with all your soul, with all your mind and with all your strength; and love others as you love yourself."

"Yes," said Jesus. "Do all that and you shall live."

The lawyer, somewhat taken aback, tried to save face by asking another question. Perhaps his conscience pricked him.

"But who are 'others'? Must I love everyone regardless?" he asked, looking puzzled.

Instead of answering directly, Jesus told him a

story, as He often did when He was teaching. Jesus's stories had a deeper meaning than most and are called parables, which means "earthly stories with a heavenly meaning." This is the story He told the lawyer.

Once, there was a man who was going from Jerusalem to Jericho, a distance of more than fifteen miles. The way was a rocky, lonely, and dangerous road infested by murderous brigands.

Suddenly, a gang of robbers sprang out from behind some rocks and attacked the man. They tore off his clothes and beat him senseless. Then they left him half dead, lying on the road in the blazing sun. His wounds were very painful. Flies bothered him and he was very thirsty. But there was no one anywhere near to come to his aid. His plight was terrible.

A while later, a priest was walking along the same road. When the wounded man heard footsteps, he opened his eyes. When he saw that the figure was a holy man, he felt a little happier. Surely here was someone who would help.

The holy man saw the wounded man, but he did not stop. He just hurried by on the other side. Perhaps he told himself he hadn't time to stop. Perhaps he was afraid robbers might attack him, too, and he didn't want to take that risk, so he kept going.

Shortly afterwards, there were more footsteps, and the wounded man's hopes rose again when he saw that a Levite was coming that way. A Levite was a helper in the temple, the sort of man who would probably help someone in distress.

But no, the Levite looked at the wounded man, and he too hurried by on the other side of the road.

Once more, the man heard the footsteps die away. The road became quiet and lonely again. He felt desperate.

Before long, the man heard footsteps of a different kind. This time, a donkey was coming down the road with a man on his back. The wounded man was disappointed to see that the rider was a Samaritan.

The Jews and the Samaritans had been enemies for a very long time. The Jews of Judah in the south hated the Samaritans, who lived in Samaria in the north. The Samaritans were a mixed race and were thought to be not wholly loyal to Israel's God.

The wounded man resigned himself. He felt sure he could not expect any help from a Samaritan, but, to his great surprise, the donkey stopped and the rider dismounted. He came over to the wounded man and looked kindly at him. He felt sorry for him and wondered what he could do to help.

Then he went back to his donkey and brought over some wine and some oil which he had with him. He put these on the man's wounds, to act as antiseptic and ointment, and bandaged him up. He probably had to tear strips off some of his own clothes in order to make bandages, as it is unlikely that he carried any with him.

Next he lifted up the wounded man gently and put him on his own donkey. Then, with the Samaritan walking at the side and holding the wounded man, they slowly made their way until they came to an inn.

The Samaritan asked the innkeeper for a room, and lead the man to it. Then he made him comfortable and left him to sleep.

The following day, the Samaritan had to continue his journey, but before he went, he took money from his purse and gave it to the innkeeper. "Look after him," he told the innkeeper, "and if it should cost you any more than this, I will pay you the extra amount when I come back this way again."

Having finished his story, Jesus turned to the lawyer and asked, "Which of these three passersby do you think acted with love to the attacked man?"

"The one who showed pity and acted kindly to him," replied the lawyer.

"Then go and do the same," said Jesus.

JESUS BLESSES THE CHILDREN

ne day, Jesus and His disciples were going to Capernaum, and on the way the disciples were arguing among themselves as to who was the greatest and most important of them.

When they arrived, Jesus questioned them about their discussion. "What were you arguing about on the way here?" He asked. However, Jesus knew, without needing any answer from them, and He sat down and called them all to Him.

"If you want to be first and really important," He said, "you must put yourself last. You must be ready to be the servant of everyone else. Those are the people who are truly great."

Now, there was a little child listening to all this — perhaps he was the child who lived in the house. Jesus put His arm around him, and said, "The greatest in the Kingdom of Heaven is one who is as humble as this little child. Anyone who welcomes a child is welcoming Me. For he who is least among you is the greatest."

Jesus was trying to explain to His disciples that God's kingdom has very different standards from the world. Riches and power do not make anyone great in God's eyes. Being loving, generous, humble, and forgiving are far more important, and people with these qualitites are the ones who are truly great. Such people may seem as unimportant as a child, but in God's kingdom, they are the ones who are greatest.

Jesus loved children. On one occasion, some people brought a group of children to Jesus. They wanted Him to put His hands on them and bless them. When the disciples saw what was happening, they rebuked the people and tried to hush the children and send them away, for they did not want Jesus to be troubled. They thought that children were not important enough to claim His attention.

Jesus, however, thought differently. He was never troubled by people coming to Him, and he would never turn anyone away.

He called the children back, saying: "Let the children come to Me, and do not try to stop them, for the Kingdom of God belongs to children such as these."

He did not mean that people should be childish and never grow up. He meant that they should receive God's kingdom in a child-like spirit – one of humble, loving trust.

THE LITTLE GIRL WHO CAME BACK

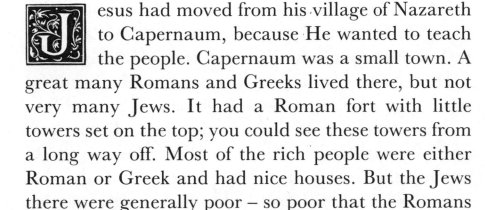esus had moved from his village of Nazareth to Capernaum, because He wanted to teach the people. Capernaum was a small town. A great many Romans and Greeks lived there, but not very many Jews. It had a Roman fort with little towers set on the top; you could see these towers from a long way off. Most of the rich people were either Roman or Greek and had nice houses. But the Jews there were generally poor – so poor that the Romans had built their synagogue for them. They all lived in friendship together.

There were, however, a few Jews in Capernaum who were well-off. Among them was the father of a little girl who loved his daughter more than anything else in the world. His name was Jairus. That is a Greek name, which he liked better than his Hebrew name of Jair. He loved everything that was wise and everything that was beautiful, and he tried to bring up his little girl to love them, too.

The country in which they lived is still, in

springtime, covered with the most beautiful wild-flowers in the world. All over the plains near her home, the little girl could see blue and yellow lupins, azure borage, anemones in red and blue and purple, pink "ragged robins," and big daisies in white and gold. The black and white storks would stand solemnly among the flowers; and the kingfishers, like living emeralds and sapphires, would flash across a little stream that flowed into the Sea of Galilee.

Here, too, would be hoopoes, with beautiful crested heads and golden-buff necks, but, oh! so untidy in their little holes in the trees. There were pretty partridges, calling to their downy chicks among the rocks; and, every now and then, a wonderful rare fishing eagle, hung with beating wings over the northern end of the lake, and then fell like a stone into the water, sending up a shower of sparkling spray in its mighty dive to catch fish in the River Jordan.

The town of Capernaum itself stood where four great roads met – roads down which caravans of people, with mules and camels, were always coming and going. There was a big pool, rather like what we call a reservoir, blue and deep, just where these four roads met; here the merchants bought and sold all kinds of things – ivory, and silk, and beautiful ornaments from a city in Syria called Damascus.

There was another narrower road there, too, which led right down to the beach of the Sea of Galilee. It passed between the houses of a fishing village called Bethsaida, which was built almost on the shore itself, while Capernaum stood higher on the hill. The young fisherman John lived in Bethsaida with his father, Zebedee, and his brother, James. Andrew and Simon Peter had their homes there, too, and so did Philip, another disciple.

Now Jairus's daughter, as she walked through the town with her father and mother, or perhaps with her Greek nursemaid, must often have seen the Lord Jesus. She must have met Him in the lanes where the palm trees and cactus grew. She almost surely would have seen Him seated a little way from the shore in Simon Peter's fishing-boat, teaching the people who thronged to the water's edge to hear Him.

In the cool evenings, she and her father would come across the Master walking quietly among the dewy flowers, wearing his long square coat of lambs' wool, with its white fringes at the corners, and its hem of blue all around. In this coat everyone immediately knew that he was a Jew. For, at this time, the people of Samaria were quite distinct from the Jewish Israelites. Jairus would have worn the same sort of coat himself. Also, they would sometimes have worn two tiny leather ornaments, one bound with a strap to the forehead and the other to the back of the right hand, called "phylacteries". They held two very small rolls of parchment, on which were written the laws that the Hebrews had to obey. Jairus would have worn his very often, for he was an important person in Capernaum and a leader in the Synagogue. But perhaps the Lord Jesus did not wear the little leather ornaments, for He lived the life of a simple carpenter or of a fisherman among the poor people of Bethsaida.

Jairus's daughter must have heard her father and mother talk a great deal about Christ. Although we know that in Jerusalem Herod lived a wicked life, and many of his courtiers did the same, in other places in Palestine there were a number of Israelites who believed that Jehovah was going to show Himself again to the Hebrews – but not in the thunder of a mountain, or the soft breezes of a dusky, star lit garden, or even in the Holy of Holies in the big Temple from which the Ark of the Covenant had been lost. They believed that, this time, a wonderful and gracious man would come forth to lead them. And they were beginning to feel sure that this man was with them now, moving among the flowers and birds of Galilee, in the person of the great teacher from Nazareth, who was called Jesus, the Christ.

The little girl would have seen John the Baptist, too, in his rough striped smock and leather girdle. She would have heard about the ford called the Upper Bethabara, where the oleanders grew, and where John had baptized Christ. And she would hear the people say that a dove, made all of golden light, had floated down with widespread wings from the sky and hung for a moment above the brows of Jesus before it flew away.

Perhaps she would go herself, breathless and wondering, to some ford of the river, and see her parents submit to this strange ceremony performed by the lion-like baptizer from the high hills – a priest of a new order of holiness. The story of the Angel Gabriel appearing to Zacharias in the Temple, and of the angels on the plains of Bethlehem, must have been told in her hearing. Her father would have read aloud the prophecies from the long parchment rolls that made up his library of books, and would have quoted the old poet's beautiful words:

"The branch of the Lord shall be beautiful and glorious."

"A man shall be as a hiding place from the wind and as a refuge from the tempest."

"The Day-spring from on high hath visited us."

"Thy dead men still live; together with my dead body shall they arise. Awake and sing, ye that dwell in dust! For thy dew is as the dew of herbs, and the earth shall cast out the dead."

"His name shall be called Wonderful, Counsellor, the mighty God, the Everlasting Father, the Prince of Peace."

It was for a Man such as this that the faithful Israelites waited so patiently, and of whom Jairus's little girl would hear so much. She must often have gone to bed with these words ringing in her ears – "Wonderful, Counsellor, the Prince of Peace." On Sabbath days, she would help her mother make her father ready for the Synagogue, which was, you know, the place where the Jews held their religious services, and where she, herself, was taught on weekdays. Jairus always put on a special blue and white scarf for this service. But the little girl would most likely have worn a simple frock like the Greek and Roman children with whom she played.

She would go to the Synagogue, and there she would sing the very psalms that people sing in our services today! How much they would mean to her! When the sweet words rang out: "In Salem also is his tabernacle, and his dwelling place in Zion!" she would think of the Temple of Jerusalem, not many miles away, to which her father and mother journeyed on high feast-days. And, at the Synagogue, she would see the Lord Jesus, with John, and James, and Zebedee; and farmhands and harvesters from the country all around. The Synagogue was very crowded in those days. Everybody pressed to see and hear this new prophet, who made deaf people hear, and blind people see, and even raised dead people to life again.

The Synagogue was a beautiful white building, rather like the buildings of Greece, with a long flight of marble steps. It must have looked very handsome among the houses around, which were made of a dark stone. Jairus's daughter may have heard Christ preach His first sermon in Galilee there; and it was not like any sermon that had ever been preached in the Synagogue before.

On the same day, a man, who, like Saul of old, was tormented by thoughts and dreams of evil, began to shout in the middle of the service, calling to Christ, this Holy One of God, to go away and leave the Evil Ones alone. But the Lord Jesus just turned His calm eyes to the place from which the shoutings came, and spoke gravely to the Evil Ones who had taken up their home in the poor man's mind. And the Spirits of Darkness fled; the man, healed and penitent, bent his head in deep gratitude before Christ, the Light of the World.

The little daughter of Jairus probably saw and heard all these things. More and more eagerly she began to question her father, and to watch in the lanes, and on the sandy shore, for the passings of the Lord Jesus. And she learned to love Him, in her childish way, very deeply. She loved His tender eyes, His sweet smile, and His beautiful, strong, kind voice. She was sorry when He went away to teach in other villages, and so glad when He came back again.

Then, one hot day, when the Lord Jesus was some miles away, in a country that belonged to people who were called the Gadarenes, the little daughter of Jairus became very sick. She lay, tossing and moaning, on her small bed, and her father and mother were in deep grief about her. Day after day, she grew worse, and at last there seemed to be no hope – everybody thought she would die. Jairus prayed, with all his heart, for the return of the Lord Jesus, because he felt sure that only the Master could save her.

The little girl was at her very worst when her father went out one day, and saw, coming across the lake, the sail of the ship that was bringing back the

Master to the shore under the city of Capernaum.

Everybody flocked to meet Him as He stepped on to the rocky beach. But Jairus was first of all. When he saw the Lord Jesus, he fell at His feet and begged Him to come to his home and save his little daughter.

The Master set off up the road, with a great crowd of people following. As they reached the house, a sobbing servant came out and said to Jairus:

"Thy daughter is dead! Trouble not the Master."

Jairus gave a low cry, but the Lord Jesus turned to him and spoke with grave tenderness.

"Fear not!" He said. "Only believe, and she shall be made well again."

Then He entered the house and went up into the room where the little, dead child was laid. People were sobbing noisily about her, but the Master held up His hand and bade them hush.

"Weep not," He said, "weep not! She is not dead, but sleepeth."

But nobody believed Him, for they felt sure she was dead. They could not understand, you see, that the Master knew her spirit was still alive, and that He had the power to call it back again to the world that it had left.

Then the Master sent them all away, all but the child's father and mother, and Peter, and James and

John. While these five stood a little way off, He went up, quite alone, to the bedside and took the little girl's cold, still hand.

"Little girl!" He said, in a sweet low voice, bending over her with, oh! such a kind loving face, "Little girl! Arise!"

A thrill ran through the quiet small body, the innocent eyes opened, and the spirit of Jairus's daughter came back. She sat up and looked, with all her old childish love, into the face of the Lord Jesus.

He put His arm around her and told her father and mother to come and kiss her again on her warm, living, little mouth. He said they were to give her something to eat, for she would soon be well. Then He went quietly from the house, telling them that they need not talk to anybody about the wonderful thing He had done.

But Jairus's daughter would often wake in the night to think of Him, and whisper to herself the words – "His Name shall be called Wonderful."

How much – how very much – those words of Isaiah must have meant to her now!

"Little girl," Jesus said, "Arise!" (page 218)

The people sang joyfully, "Hosanna! Hosanna!" (page 227)

JESUS THE HEALER

esus soon became well-known for His works of healing and people came to him from far and near to be cured of their illness.

One day, after he had been teaching in Galilee, there came to Him a man who was suffering from a terrible skin disease called leprosy. Today it is possible to cure this disease, but in Jesus's day there was no hope at all. A leper had to keep away from other people because the law regarded him as unclean. No one, knowing him to be a leper would dare approach him, but if anyone accidentally did come near him, the leper had to cry out "Unclean!" and people would hastily back away in case they caught the disease.

Thus lepers, as well as being ill, led a very lonely life, entirely cut off from human company, except for other lepers.

But Jesus did not shun them, for He never shunned anyone in trouble. When this leper came and asked to be healed, Jesus stretched out His hand

and touched him. The leper said, "If you will, you can make me clean."

"I will," said Jesus. "Be clean," and immediately the disease left the man.

Jesus often made blind men see again, and one day, outside Jericho, a blind man sat by the roadside. His name was Bartimaeus.

Many blind people have a keen sense of hearing, and Bartimaeus would have been able to recognize the familiar sounds of people and animals passing by. He would also have heard about the great healer, Jesus of Nazareth.

One day, Bartimaeus heard the noise of a great crowd of people coming along the road, such a noise as he had never heard before. He could tell, from the scraps of conversation he heard, that Jesus was with them. He could not see Jesus, of course, but he wondered if Jesus could see him. He decided to call out and attract His attention. "Jesus, son of David, have mercy on me!" he cried.

People in the crowd scolded him. "Be quiet!" they said.

But Bartimaeus cried out all the more loudly, "Son of David, have mercy on me!" Calling him "son of David" showed that Bartimaeus had given some thought as to who Jesus really was.

Jesus stopped and said to the people, "Call him."

So they called to him and said, "Take heart; get up, for Jesus is calling you."

Bartimaeus jumped up and made his way to Jesus.

"What do you want me to do?" Jesus asked.

"Lord, that I might receive my sight," answered Bartimaeus.

"Go your way," said Jesus, "your faith has made you whole."

At once Bartimaeus was able to see, and he followed Jesus along the road.

Another time, Jesus healed a man in Jerusalem. There was a pool in that city with five porches or porticoes; it was called the Pool of Bethesda. This pool, with its five porticoes, has since been discovered by archaeologists, down below the level of present-day Jerusalem.

A large number of sick people used to lie in the porches waiting for the waters to become stirred up or "troubled." This happened from time to time, perhaps caused by the bubbling up of an underground stream, but the people believed that the first to go into the water when it was bubbling would be cured of his or her illness.

When Jesus went there, He saw, among the crowds of sick people, one man who had been ill for thirty-eight years. He was lying on a mat and seemed to be the sort of person who had lost all will to live.

"Do you really want to get well?" asked Jesus, stopping beside him.

"Sir," replied the man, "I have no one to help me into the pool when the water is troubled, and while I am struggling to get in, someone else always gets there first, and I lose my chance."

Obviously, the man needed encouragement.

"Get up, pick up your mat, and walk!" said Jesus to him. Immediately, the man found that he could stand. He picked up his mat and started to walk. When he realized that he was cured, he knelt before Jesus and thanked him before walking away to start a new and healthy life.

THE CHILDREN WHO CRIED "HOSANNA!"

Jesus had finished His work on the shores of Galilee, where the beautiful red oleanders blossomed near the shining waters of the lake. Because He wished to go to Jerusalem, He walked quietly and steadily towards the city on the hills following the windings of the River Jordan, and healing sick people as He went. Everyone who knew that He was passing flocked to see and hear Him; mothers and fathers brought their little children to be blessed. Jesus loved the babies, and their toddling brothers and sisters. He took them up in His kind arms, and laid His hand on their heads and blessed each one.

By and by, He came close to Jerusalem and went up a long, dusty road to a cool silver-green wood on the top of a hill. The trees there were olives, and so the hill was called Mount Olivet. It was soft and beautiful in the shade there, and on the opposite hilltop, you could see the snow-white marble walls and the glittering brass gates of the holy Temple

225

shining in the sun. The Master looked at Jerusalem with His face full of love and longing. Then He said to two of His disciples:

"Go to the village that is just over there. As you enter, you will find a donkey tied up by the road, and a colt with her, on which no man has ever ridden. Untie them and bring them to Me, and if anybody asks why you do such a thing, say, 'The Lord hath need of them.' And he will immediately agree to send them to Me."

The two disciples went down the road and presently came to a little house where two paths met. Beside the door of the little house were tied a gentle mother donkey and a beautiful big young colt, with bright eyes, soft skin, and ears pricked forward. The disciples began to untie the mother donkey, but the people to whom she belonged came up and asked, "What do ye, loosing the colt?"

The disciples looked into the surprised faces, and just said quietly, "The Lord hath need of them." Then the owners of the donkey and the colt were only too glad to let their animals be used by the loving and gracious Master. The two disciples led the mother donkey away, while the beautiful young colt trotted contentedly behind. And they all disappeared into the silvery shadows of the olive trees on the hill top where they knew Jesus was waiting for them.

Very quickly, news ran through the village that the Master was near and was going into Jerusalem. The people began to gather, some hurrying out of their houses, coming around the brow of the hill, some running from the orange groves and vineyards. Soon a great crowd collected on the steep slope of the hill, waiting breathlessly for the Lord Jesus to pass. And, as they waited, suddenly a sweet faint sound of singing came to them from the distance.

This was the song the people sang:

"Hosanna! Hosanna!

"Blessed is He that cometh in the name of the Lord!

"Hosanna! Hosanna!

"Blessed be the Kingdom of our father David, that cometh in the name of the Lord!

"Hosanna in the highest!

"Hosanna! Hosanna! Hosanna!"

The song rose higher and higher. Then through the middle of the parted crowd, between the waving boughs that the men and women had gathered, came the strong, bright-eyed colt; and on the back of the colt rode the Master.

It was all very wonderful and beautiful. The people were dressed in bright clothes. Some held up olive branches, while others waved boughs of citron, or orange, with yellow gleaming fruit and fragrant white or purple flowers. As the Lord Jesus drew nearer, the men and women threw their cloaks upon the dusty road and made a soft carpet. Then they spread olive branches and myrtle boughs, on the top of the carpet. Little children ran forward and dropped their offerings of flowers; and all the time the people sang their song of "Hosanna," like a memory of the angel's music near Bethlehem many years ago.

Down this bright-hued road of song and fragrance, the Master, seated on a lovely blue and white garment that was spread on the colt's back instead of a saddle, rode quietly on.

All at once, there was a moment's hush; and, through the hush, another great song floated across the valley. The crowd on the side of Mount Olivet saw a second crowd coming down the hill from Jerusalem, towards the little river called Kedron that ran between the city and the Mount of Olives. These people were singing "Hosanna" too, but instead of branches of trees, they carried green palm leaves, such as were brought out only for great processions. Their hymn of welcome to the Lord Jesus made music in the valley, so that the rush and ripple of the brook could not be heard above their song.

Then, all of them, men, women, and children, went up the steep streets of the hill towards the Temple, the Master riding in their midst.

He dismounted from the gentle colt and went into the building that was so lovely with its snow-white pillars and its gates like shining gold. Then the little children grouped themselves all over the court where, years before, Simeon had blessed the baby Jesus. They gathered near the glittering brass Gate Beautiful and waved their myrtle-flowers and their orange boughs and sang their brave "Hosannas" more earnestly and joyfully than ever.

But, once again, there were people who asked the Master to hush the children. This time it was the Chief Priests and the Scribes who were angry because the children sang of Christ as the "Son of David." For this meant that the Master was the King. But the Lord Jesus looked at the children tenderly and smiled in answer to their song.

"Nay!" He told the priests, "nay! Do you not know that long ago the words were written, 'Out of the mouths of little children comes to the most perfect praise?' "

THE LAST SUPPER

uring the week which began with that first Palm Sunday, Passover was celebrated all over Israel. Jesus and His disciples were in Jerusalem to celebrate the festival.

Jesus gave special instructions to two of His disciples. "Go into the city," He said. "A man carrying a pitcher of water will meet you both there. Follow him into the house which he enters, and ask in which room I am to eat the Passover with my disciples. He will show you an upper room. Then I want you to prepare the Passover meal there. The rest of us will join you later."

The two disciples went and found everything as Jesus had said. That evening, which was Thursday, Jesus and His disciples assembled in the upper room. The disciples did not know it then, but this was to be no ordinary Passover meal. Jesus was about to transform it into the Lord's Supper – a meal which has been continued in Christian churches all over the world ever since.

When the supper had been served, Jesus rose from the table. He took off His outer robe and tied a towel around His waist. Then He poured water in a basin and did a job which in those days was usually performed by a slave – He began to wash the disciples' feet.

The disciples had been arguing over which of them was the most important. None of them had wanted the menial job of feet-washing at the supper for fear of being thought less important than the others. So when no one offered to perform this courteous act, Jesus rose and willingly did it Himself for the whole company.

When He came to Simon Peter, that disciple protested, "You shall never wash my feet, Lord. It is not right."

"If I do not," said Jesus, "you have no part of me."

Jesus meant this symbolically – unless He washed Peter's sins from him, he had no link with Jesus.

Then Peter, perhaps beginning to understand, said, "Lord, not only my feet, but also my hands and my head."

When Jesus had washed all the disciples' feet, He returned to His place at the table and sat down facing them all.

Then He said, "You call me teacher and Lord, and

you are right to do so, for that is what I am. But if I, your Lord and teacher, have washed your feet, so ought you to follow my example and wash one another's feet."

He was teaching them that truly great people do not put themselves first, but serve others.

As they were eating, Jesus said something startling. "I tell you truly," He said, "that one of you will betray me."

The disciples were puzzled and looked at one another in alarm, each thinking, "Surely He cannot mean me." Peter motioned to the disciple who was sitting next to Jesus (most likely John) to ask Him whom he meant. The disciple asked Him quietly, and Jesus replied, "It is the one to whom I give a piece of bread which I have dipped in the sauce of this dish."

Then He took a piece of bread, dipped it, and gave it to Judas Iscariot. It was Jesus's last appeal to Judas, but Judas rejected it.

"Do quickly what you are about to do," said Jesus to Judas. Again the disciples did not understand what Jesus meant, for they did not know that Judas was going to betray their master.

During the meal, Jesus took a piece of bread and said a prayer of thanks. Then He broke the bread and gave it to His disciples saying, "Take and eat; this is My body which is given for you."

Then He took a cup of wine, gave thanks to God, and handed it to them saying, "This is My blood which is poured out for many for the forgiveness of sins. Do this in memory of Me."

After Judas had left, Jesus spoke again to the disciples and tried to help them to understand why His death had to happen. "I shall not be with you for very much longer," He said, "and you cannot come where I am going. Now I give you a new commandment, that you love one another. If you act in this way, then everyone will know that you are my disciples."

"Why can't I follow you now?" asked Peter. "I am ready to die for you."

"Are you?" said Jesus sadly. "I tell you that before the cock crows, you will have said three times that you did not know Me."

"I'll never say that," said Peter stoutly, "even if I have to die with you."

And the other disciples said the same, protesting their loyalty to Jesus.

Jesus told them much else about what was to happen. He would be returning to His Father and preparing the way for others to come to Him, too.

"THIS DAY SHALT THOU BE WITH ME IN PARADISE"

oon there came a strange, sad day for the people, and, above all, for the children of Jerusalem.

You know that those who followed, and were faithful to the Lord Jesus, loved to call Him their King and the son of David. The priests at Jerusalem in those days were not men who wanted to keep the glory of the Temple pure for the worship of Jehovah. They sought office, and the wealth and power of office, for themselves alone. They were always careful not to displease the Romans, who governed Palestine then. So they said to each other:

"If we go to Pontius Pilate, the Roman Governor, we can tell him that there is a carpenter from Nazareth calling Himself the King of the Jews. If the Governor knows that the people are listening to Jesus and supporting Him, and that they will very likely rise in rebellion under His leading, then Pilate will have Him put to death!"

So the priests began to look everywhere in

Jerusalem for the Lord Jesus. Guided by the disciple, Judas Iscariot, they found Him in a garden in Gethsemane through which a little river flowed. Their soldiers took Him prisoner, and led Him before Pontius Pilate, who was visiting Jerusalem at the time of the great Passover feast.

Many people had come to Jerusalem for the Passover, and among them would certainly have been Jairus and his wife. I think it is most likely that they would have brought with them their little daughter who had been restored to life. She must have been doubly precious to them now. She could never again be quite like other children, for she had glanced inside the glass of Paradise.

She and her father and mother would have stayed with friends in the Holy City, for there were no hotels, as we understand them, in Jerusalem. But very few of the rich people followed and loved the Master; and nobody was powerful enough to save Him when the High Priests told Pontius Pilate that He was going to lead a rebellion against the Roman rulers.

Among the very few who really did understand that Kingdom of which Christ spoke so lovingly as He trod among the flowers or through the quiet woods, was a rich Jew called Joseph of Arimathea.

He had a house with a beautiful garden around it. It is very likely, though we really do not know, that Jairus and his wife, with their little girl, could have spent Passover in Jerusalem as the guests of Joseph of Arimathea.

Now, think of one child who perhaps knew more about death than anybody else in the world – the little girl who had come back to her father and mother from Paradise, and who may, on that sad day when the Holy Jesus was nailed to a Cross to die, have been wandering quietly by herself in the beautiful garden of Joseph of Arimathea.

It was a lovely time of the year, and the fullness of spring must have been in the garden, all sweet and blue with iris below, and pale and pink with almond blossom above. As the child walked there, she must have heard the footsteps of a sad-hearted crowd outside. Then, perhaps another child would run quickly into the garden, and, all bewildered, would tell her that men were killing the Master – putting nails into His hands and feet, and setting Him upon a high Cross, so that He must die. And I can think that Jairus's little daughter would hold out her own small hands and look at them thoughtfully.

"There were no nails through my hands, you know," she might say, "but everybody thought I was

"Yes, I am sure that He will come back" (page 241)

"Why seek ye the living among the dead?" (page 244)

dead, did they not?"

And the other child would answer wonderingly, "Yes."

Then it would begin to grow dim in the garden, for there was a great darkness over Jerusalem when the Master died. But to Jairus's little daughter there was no darkness in death – nothing but the fair light of that distant place in which her soul had wandered for a few hours.

"Has the Master said anything?" she might ask.

And would not the child tell her then of the wonderful words of promise and hope given to a poor thief who was nailed to another cross by the Master's side?

"Today shalt thou be with Me in Paradise."

The little girl who had herself come back from Paradise must have known something of what it was like.

John, too, must have heard those strange and beautiful words as he stood with Mary, Christ's mother, leaning on his young shoulder, by the sad and holy cross. Long afterwards, when he was quite an old man, prisoner on an island, John, too, had a vision of the Paradise to which the Master promised to show the dying thief the way.

So the little daughter of Jairus would go on smiling

dreamily in the garden as the shadows closed in, deeper and deeper, upon the earth. I think, perhaps, when the darkness was at its deepest, she would fall fast asleep, so that when the other child came back, pale with sorrow, she would open her eyes in quiet joy, and the other child would look at her in wonder.

"The Master is dead," the child would tell her. "I asked why they had killed Him, and they told me because He wanted to be our King – and Caesar is King!"

But would not Jairus's little daughter know better?

"The Master *is* our King," she would answer. "And He is not dead. I have been asleep under the olive trees! I seemed to go back into that beautiful country where I was when I was thought to be dead. The angels were there – oh, so many, standing and listening! It was twilight, and I saw a long path with flowers. Then a great star seemed to hang over the path – you remember the star when the Master was born? Then, through the light of the Star, He came! He smiled at me, just as He smiled always on the shore at home. He had a crown of thorns on, you said, a little while ago. It had turned into a crown of stars, and there were roses in His hands, so that you could not see the wounds. I think a little angel child had laid them there as He came up the path. He is not dead – any more than *I* was dead."

"But will He come back? Oh, will He come back?"

And Jairus's little daughter would answer: "Yes. I am *quite sure* that, for a little time, He will come back – just as I came back."

THE FIRST EASTER

any of the people of Jerusalem said that the Master was dead and would never come back to the hills of Galilee or the woods of Olivet.

Joseph of Arimathea had taken His body from the cross and had laid it reverently in the rocky cave in the garden where, in the last story, we imagined Jairus's daughter might have sat. Soldiers were assigned to guard it, and the women who had loved the Lord Jesus had watched, weeping, as a great stone was rolled into the opening of the cave, so that the inside was all closed up and dark. Then the women had gone away, down the road to their homes in Jerusalem; and Mary, the mother of Jesus, had been taken by John to a quiet house there – a house that must have belonged to his relations in the city. Simon Peter had gone with John, for, as you know, they were great friends.

So the night passed quietly, and the next day, which was the Jewish Sabbath, was spent by everybody in rest. But on the third night, a strange and wonderful thing happened.

Roman soldiers had kept watch ever since the cave had been sealed up with the stone. They had grown tired with their long vigil, and had fallen asleep. All at once, through the dark stillness of the garden, came a long, low rumbling, like an earthquake.

It echoed among the dark cypresses, and across the valley that ran right through the very heart of Jerusalem. It roused the soldiers, and they were very frightened. Then, after a few minutes, the sound died completely away.

No light was showing yet in the east, but presently, coming along the road from the place where the dark roofs of the houses clustered, there might have been seen the lights of three lanterns. They twinkled like fireflies in the distance, and came nearer and nearer to the garden. They were carried by three women – Mary, the mother of James, and another who was called Salome, and Mary Magdalene, who had followed the Lord Jesus from her home near Capernaum. They came towards the garden in the darkness, talking together very sadly, and bringing spices in little bowls, with which they meant to sprinkle the soft, white linen clothes in which the body of the Master had been wrapped before it was placed in the little cave.

They entered the gate and went inside, stepping softly over the grass and among the tall black cypress trees, wondering to each other in whispers whom they could find to roll away the big stone. So they reached the rocky part of the garden where the body of Christ had been laid.

When they got there, they saw that the stone had already been rolled away, and that the Roman soldiers were crouched and huddled up with fear. Lifting their lanterns, the women looked inside the open cave and saw that it was still and empty, with only the linen burial clothes lying where the body of Jesus had rested three days ago.

Mary Magdalene turned quickly away, sobbing with grief. She thought someone has stolen the body of Christ, and she ran back to the town to tell the disciples. The other women stood, hushed and troubled, beside the cave, asking each other in low voices what could have happened. As they talked, all at once there was a great shining in the dark garden, and they saw that an angel was seated on the stone, and that others were inside the cave.

The angels gave the women the first Easter message:

"Why seek ye the living among the dead? He is not

here, but is risen! Remember how He spake unto you while He was yet in Galilee!"

Then the shining angels told the women to go and give the disciples these tidings of joy.

* * * * * *

Mary Magdalene had already wakened Peter and John, and they, too, were hurrying through the dark morning towards the garden. When they got there, everything was again still and deserted. The excited women had hastened off in different directions, and the terrified Roman soldiers had fled. Peter and John looked into the cave and saw that it was empty except for the linen clothes, just as Mary Magdalene had said. But they did not see the angels, and they went back home, wondering and disturbed.

Only Mary Magdalene stayed on in the garden.

Dawn was beginning to break now, showing clear and pale among the trees. The blue rock doves that had their nests quite close to the little cave began to murmur and coo, and the flowers smelled sweeter than ever. But Mary Magdalene noticed none of these things. Her lantern had gone out, her long robe was wet with dew, and her tears fell on the bowl of spices which she still held in her hands. She was nearly heartbroken because she could not find the body of the Lord.

Then there came again the wonderful shining inside the cave. And she, too, stooped and saw the angels.

They asked why she wept. She answered that it was because she did not know where people had laid the body of her dear Master.

At that moment, she heard a movement behind, and a gentle voice asked why she was crying. She thought it must be the gardener speaking and begged him to tell her if *he* knew where the Master's body had been laid. Then the figure at which she gazed through the tears became clearer, and the eyes that met hers were full of love. The Master's own tender tones fell on her ears.

"Mary!" he said.

Just one word, but she knew! As she fell on her knees and prayed, the full morning broke. There stood the living Lord Jesus, in the glory of the sunshine, with the dewy flowers opening their petals wide around Him, and the larks soaring towards heaven, pouring out their souls in song.

HE IS RISEN!

o you want to know where the Lord Jesus went first of all, after He rose from death in the garden of Joseph of Arimathea?

Well, I think He went to visit the different places in the countryside where He had healed the sick and made the lame to walk.

Because this is the story of what happened later on that first wonderful Easter Day.

All the disciples in Jerusalem were telling each other what Mary Magdalene had seen. You know that a number of visitors had gone to Jerusalem for the Passover Feast – and it was the first day of the week in the city as well. Late in the afternoon, everybody started, as usual, to go back home. Among them were two disciples from a little village called Emmaus, which was built in the middle of the grassy plains three-score furlongs, or about six miles, from Jerusalem.

These two talked very earnestly as they walked towards their home, carrying their empty baskets.

They knew all about the Lord Jesus of Nazareth, and were among those who had heard Him teach and had seen Him cure the sick with a touch and a word. They knew, too, that those who hated Him had tried to kill Him because those who loved Him called Him the King.

They reminded each other of the wonderful star that had appeared in Bethlehem thirty-three years before, and of the angels among the olive trees, and of the Wise Men who came to worship the little baby.

As they talked, they saw a stranger coming towards them over the plain from the direction of Jerusalem.

The stranger joined them, asking what they were talking about so earnestly and why they were so sad. They told Him that the Lord Jesus, who, they believed, was the little baby the angels had sung about, and who they had thought would be the great King promised to the Jews, had been crucified; and that though His body had gone away, and Mary Magdalene said she had seen Him alive again, yet nobody else had done so, and they found the story hard to believe. The stranger looked at them with wise wonderful eyes and began to talk.

He told them many things about the promised King, and they began to understand that there were two Kingdoms – one with a palace and a garden that they could see – like Herod's – and another with many palaces and gardens that they could not see – like the lovely place the daughter of Jairus had dreamed about. As the stranger talked, they reached the village, and the disciples begged Him to come in and have supper, for the night was coming on.

He went in with them and sat down to supper. Taking a piece of bread, He said grace. Then He broke the bread, and gave to each of them a piece. As He did so, a change seemed to come over Him; and they saw that He was no stranger, but the Lord Jesus Himself. As they gazed in amazement, He vanished out of their sight.

They could not wait then to finish their supper, but put on their cloaks, took their sticks in their hands, and hurried out into the night to go back and tell the disciples at Jerusalem. As they went out into the starlight, they looked across the shadowy pastures that lay on every side.

Shepherds were there, as usual, with their sheep. And though the angels did not come to the plains of Palestine that night, I think the echo of their song came back among the stars:

"Glory to God in the highest, and on earth peace, goodwill to men!"

THE FIRELIGHT ON THE SHORE OF GALILEE

The young fisher, John, whom Jesus loved so much, was seated in the bow of a ship that rocked softly on the sea. It was a very still night, with a soft, dark sky, sparkling with thousands of stars. The nets were spread on the left-hand side of the boat, but, so far, the fishermen had not caught anything. John, looking out into the starry darkness, was dreaming and thinking of the Lord Jesus. All the disciples knew now that He had risen from the dead, for they had more than once seen Him and spoken to Him. John was wishing very much that He would show Himself again. He missed the Master very much, though it was a deep joy to know that He was alive again.

As John sat in the boat, watching the stars high above the dark hills, suddenly he saw a little glow of red light among the shadows on the shore. It showed all clear and crimson for a moment, not much larger than a flower. Then it spread and widened, throwing a lovely brightness on the ripples that broke close at hand. John now saw that it was a small, steady fire made of charcoal; and he thought he could discern the shadowy figure of a man standing near, feeding the flame.

As John watched, a feeling of deep awe and gladness came over him. He felt sure, somehow, that it was the Lord Himself. He believed this, because Christ had promised to come to Galilee. Then all the fishermen heard a clear voice, calling through the darkness and over the water:

"Children! Have you anything to eat?"

At that moment, dawn began to break.

The fishermen could not see the face of that dim, mysterious figure by the fire on the edge of the sea, and they did not know who it was. They called out, rather sorrowfully, that, so far, they had not caught any fish at all. In reply, the voice came over the water again:

"Throw your nets over the right-hand side of the boat!"

The fishermen hauled up their nets as quickly as they could, and let them out again on the other side of the ship. At once, the nets were filled with bright, gleaming fishes.

John knew then, for certain, who stood on the shore by the little fire in the growing light. He said to Peter under his breath: "It is the Lord!"

Peter gave a low exclamation of wonder and joy. Then he jumped straight out of the boat into the shallow water and waded to the shore in haste to worship Christ again. The other fishermen started rowing towards the land, dragging the heavy, fish-laden nets after them; and Simon Peter, who, after all, had not yet dared to speak to the shadowy figure on the beach, helped them draw the nets to land.

The nets were full and shining with fishes, looking as if they were covered with silver as they lay on the pale, dawn-lit pebbles. Yet the nets were not broken. The fishermen climbed, one by one, out of the boat and drew nearer to the Lord Jesus, as He stood quietly by the small bright fire. Then they saw that He had been preparing food for them – broiling fish on the charcoal, and dividing little loaves of bread. Then, although they were still too awed to speak, He talked to them.

"Come and dine." Then He gave them the fish and the bread, just as He had given food to the crowds of people out of the little boy's basket up in the very hills that, tipped with the light of morning, surrounded them now.

John crept nearer to the Lord Jesus in the growing brightness, and at last the lad was nestling close to

Him again, his heart almost bursting with gladness and love.

For a long time, the Master sat and talked with the fishermen, as He used to do in the days that had passed. He said more, perhaps, to Simon Peter than to any of the others. Three times He asked him, as if half in doubt, "Simon, son of Jonas, lovest thou Me?" And Peter, grieved, answered that Christ must know he loved Him. And then Jesus told Peter to feed His sheep and His lambs – the grown-up people, and the children, who would believe in His word in all the long years to come.

* * * * * *

Jesus showed Himself again to the disciples after this, when they were back in Jerusalem. He came to them as they sat quietly talking at supper and taught them once more. Then He rose and told them to come with Him towards Bethany.

Do you remember the brook where the children gathered the myrtles, and the stony mountainside that had once rung with "Hosannas" as Christ rode down upon the donkey? This was the way He led the disciples now. They followed Him across the stream, up into the flowery slopes above. Then He turned

His loving face towards them, held up His hands, and blessed them. As they knelt to receive the blessing, some of them might have seen a soft golden cloud come over the hilltop, drifting through the silver olive boughs, and lying, delicately lovely, upon the grass and flowers. This golden cloud perhaps floated over the figure of the Master; His robes, His hands and His face would look bright and shining beneath it. At last, He seemed to be folded into the very heart of the glory, and it was as if there were angels' wings around Him, drawing Him up to the sky.

When the mist floated softly away, the Master had vanished. Out of the bosom of the golden cloud, He had gone back home to God.

Jesus stood on the shore beside the fire (page 252)

While He blessed them, He was parted from them (page 254)

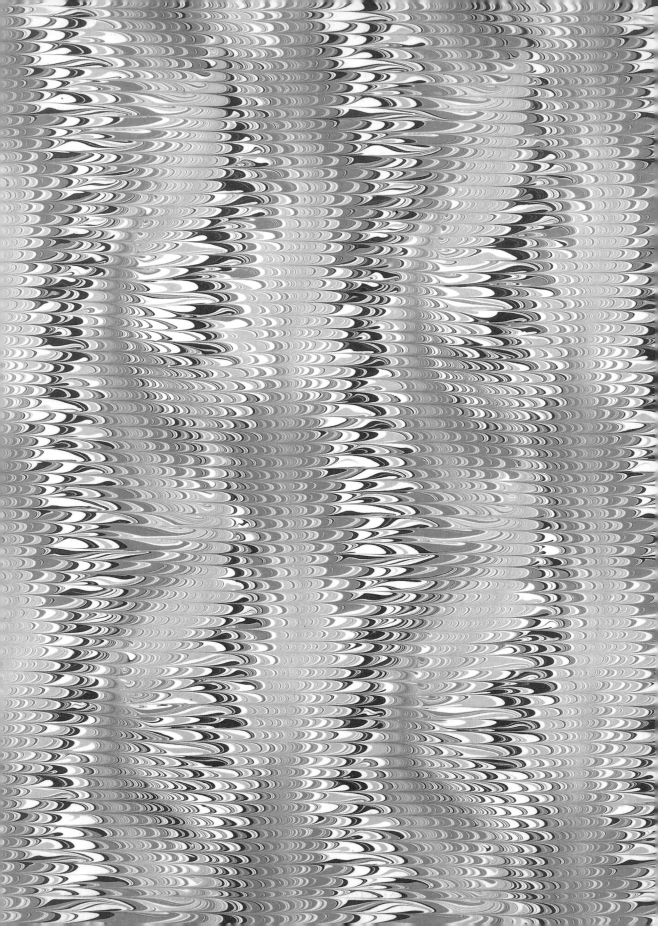